When one views the heroic, uncompromising Mr. Valiant-for-truth, the self-forgetful, issue-driven Controversialist, the ever-public proclaimer of the Bible, the laughing humorist, the ever-flowing stream of edifying literature that was Charles Spurgeon, it is difficult to fit into that profile a man so thoroughly and consistently engulfed in mental and spiritual pain and depression. Yet, the fully-dimensioned Spurgeon from early years to final days found dark distress ever hovering on the edges of his mind and sometimes launching an all out assault on his very being. How he managed all this, by the grace of God, both for himself and for others, drives both the gripping content and the riveting literary style of Zack Eswine in *Spurgeon's Sorrows*. Showing both comprehensive and deep knowledge of the sermonic literature Spurgeon produced on this subject, this book is for those in such dark times, those that would seek to understand and help them, and those who have suffered life-changing loss through the inability of someone to escape the clutches of such deceitful darkness.

Tom J. Nettles
Professor of Historical Theology,
The Southern Baptist Theological Seminary, Louisville, Kentucky

Zack Eswine, like Spurgeon, a preacher, pastor, and no stranger to suffering, has immersed himself in Spurgeon's nineteenth century sermons and his experiences of depression to show us a man like ourselves, vulnerable to all sorts of difficulties and losses in life, wrestling with the eternal big questions of the goodness of God, the presence of evil and the fragility of body, mind and emotions. There is much encouragement, comfort and practical help to be found in this rich and poetic treasure.

Richard Winter
Author of *When Life Goes Dark: Finding Hope in the Midst of Depression*,
Director of Counseling, Covenant Theological Seminary, St. Louis, Missouri

Zack Eswine is a pastor with the mind of a scholar and the heart of a poet. His wisdom gleaned from Charles Spurgeon's struggle with depression is theologically profound and pastorally lucid. Recommend it to anyone you know who has wondered about depression, about pastoral ministry, or about God.

Jason Byassee
Author of *Discerning the Body: Searching for Jesus in the World*,
Senior Pastor, Boone United Methodist Church, Boone, North Carolina

The river of life often flows through sloughs of despond. Charles Spurgeon knew that well. He knew depression. He knew the God from whom life flows. Ditto Zack Eswine in this unusual, refreshing, sensible book. It is a riff and meditation on Spurgeon's experience. Eswine continually orients to the reality that depression remains an intrinsically human experience for Spurgeon. Too often in our day, depression gets reinterpreted as a "thing," is objectified into a merely medical diagnosis, is alienated from our humanness. This book shows a good way forward—no reductionistic explanations, no magic answers. Read it, and take it to heart.

David Powlison
CCEF Executive Director,
Senior Editor, Journal of Biblical Counseling, Glenside, Pennsylvania

I have known of Spurgeon for years, as a gifted and godly preacher, and like most preachers have thought, "I could never preach like that." But until I read this book I had no idea that Spurgeon was also a melancholy, that he could lift crowds to the heights, yet also himself be brought low in his despondent moods. I can say, "I can hurt like that." What a comfort to know that a great man was very human, a "man of like passions." The grace that came through his preaching also lifted his soul. It is a comfort to be reminded of that great grace.

Leighton Ford
President, Leighton Ford Ministries,
Charlotte, North Carolina

If you find yourself facing "the dark night of the soul" (or caring for someone who is), this book will help you look up and see the stars – the light shining through heaven's floor – and inspire you with the fierce hope that comes from knowing the dawn is surely coming. Poetic, poignant, and platitude-free, this shimmering treasure of a book may literally save your life or the life of someone you love.

Ken Shigematsu
Author of the best-selling *God in My Everything*
Senior Pastor, Tenth Church, Vancouver, Canada

In an age of quick answers Spurgeon speaks beyond the grave with heart-felt understanding and solace. Those who know the pain of such suffering find in these pages a level of succour for the soul which both normalizes and gives hope. We also see in Jesus one who has been this way and knows how to offer comfort.

Those who draw near as helpers find they are called upon to offer the very grace and kindness which God shows to his people. As God sympathises with us in our troubles so we are shown what true sympathy looks like.

The author of this book has given a rare insight into the experience of a ubiquitous problem. As such there is a rich blessing to be found in *Spurgeon's Sorrows*.

Margaret Reynolds
Counselor and Co-Founder of Grace Counselling & Conciliation Services,
Auckland, New Zealand

Zack Eswine's beautifully crafted *Spurgeon's Sorrows* is poetry for the soul. Weaving Spurgeon's acquaintance with depression with his own, Zack gives language to the honest struggle of the weary. He kindly invites sufferers, and their fellow sojourners, to breathe what is true, offering grace-filled help and real hope. An exquisite book.

Patti Hawley
Licensed Professional Counselor
Faculty Adjunct, Covenant Theological Seminary, St Louis, Missouri

You can almost taste Spurgeon's tears in this book. Depression is a barely understood, silent assassin in the church. If you, like me, have succumbed to this debilitating disease, then Zack Eswine's gentle, poetic, unmasking of Spurgeon's inner turmoil may become a soothing balm for your soul. It may not heal you, but a healthy empathy emerges when you read about the struggles of a man who has walked down the same dark alleys you stumble along, and somehow found God in the valley of despair. If you don't struggle with depression yourself, it will help you love those who do!

Jeremy McQuoid
Teaching Pastor, Deeside Christian Fellowship,
Aberdeen, Scotland

Spurgeon's Sorrows, a unique and timely volume from the pen of Zack Eswine, pulls from the works of Charles Spurgeon his words on a subject that can no longer be ignored because of its sweeping impact on believers and all of Christendom. Depression has moved beyond a series of bad days and seems to grip the hearts of many who claim the name and power of Christ just as did the great Victorian preacher.

The hope for all who experience this challenge personally or within the circle of family and friends is articulated well by Spurgeon and might be summarized in this way: "What he found of Jesus in the darkness can serve as a light for our own darkness." I commend this volume as one worthy of a read, especially by pastors and counselors and by any who suffer from the throes of despair.

Paige Patterson
President,
Southwestern Baptist Theological Seminary, Fort Worth, Texas

There are few men I trust more to write a book on depression than Zack Eswine. His tears have freed me to embrace my tears, and his story of heartache has taken me further into my own. So Zack hasn't merely written a book chronicling Spurgeon's often debilitating struggles with melancholy and depression; he has given us a grace-full en ramp to understand *our* sorrows, and an incredibly practical guide for caring for heart-pained friends God places in our lives. I cannot wait to buy many copies of this book to give to strugglers and caregivers alike.

Scotty Ward Smith
Teacher in Residence,
West End Community Church, Nashville, Tennessee

Spurgeon's Sorrows

Realistic Hope for those who Suffer from Depression

ZACK ESWINE

CHRISTIAN
FOCUS

Unless otherwise indicated, Scripture quotations are from The Holy Bible, *English Standard Version*, copyright © 2001 by Crossway Bibles, a division of Good News Publishers. Used by permission. All rights reserved. ESV Text Edition: 2007.

Scripture quotations marked KJV are taken from the *King James Version*. All rights reserved.

Some Scripture quotations taken directly from Spurgeon's writings reflect the *King James Version* but are worded slightly differently. They have been left as Spurgeon wrote them.

Zack Eswine was Assistant Professor of Homiletics and Director for Doctor of Ministry for six years at Covenant Theological Seminary, St Louis, Missouri. He is now Lead Pastor of Riverside Church, St Louis, Missouri. He also wrote *Kindled Fire: How the methods of C.H. Spurgeon can help your preaching* (ISBN 978-1-84550-117-4).

Copyright © Zack Eswine 2014

paperback ISBN 978-1-78191-538-7
epub ISBN 978-1-78191-543-1
mobi ISBN 978-1-78191-548-6

10 9 8 7 6 5 4 3 2 1

Printed in 2014
Reprinted twice in 2015, and once in 2016 and 2017
by
Christian Focus Publications Ltd.,
Geanies House, Fearn, Ross-shire,
IV20 1TW, Scotland, UK.
www.christianfocus.com

Cover design by Daniel van Straaten

Printed and bound by
Bell and Bain, Glasgow

MIX
Paper from
responsible sources
FSC
www.fsc.org
FSC® C007785

CONTENTS

For Jessica,

a Help in the Slough of Despond; my Hopeful friend against Giant Despair and Doubting Castle.

Acknowledgments

I also give thanks to the congregation of Riverside Church out of which I write this book. In particular, I am indebted to the time, partnership and counsel of Jonathan and Liz Block, Sam and Greta Coalier, Ray and Donna Hagerty-Payne, Jason and Natalie Wilson, Margaret Wolfinbarger. Together with Dr. Richard Winter, you have helped me grow.

"I am the subject of depressions of spirit so fearful that I hope none of you ever get to such extremes of wretchedness as I go to."[1]

"We very speedily care for bodily diseases; they are too painful to let us slumber in silence: and they soon urge us to seek a physician or a surgeon for our healing. Oh, if we were as much alive to the more serious wounds of our inner man."[2]

"Personally I know that there is nothing on earth that the human frame can suffer to be compared with despondency and prostration of mind."[3]

—Charles Haddon Spurgeon

1   Charles Spurgeon, "Joy and Peace in Believing," *Metropolitan Tabernacle Pulpit (MTP)*, Vol. 12, Sermon 692 (http://www.spurgeongems.org/vols10-12/chs692.pdf), accessed 12/14/13.

2   Charles Spurgeon, "Healing for the Wounded," *The New Park Street Pulpit (NPSP)*, Sermon 53 in *The Spurgeon Archive* (http://www.spurgeon.org/sermons/0053.htm), accessed 12/13/13.

3   Charles Spurgeon, "The Garden of the Soul," *MTP*, Vol. 12 (Ages Digital Library, 1998), p. 370.

Part One:

Trying to Understand Depression

1

The Road to Sorrow

The Road to sorrow has been well trodden,
it is the regular sheep track to heaven,
and all the flock of God have had to pass along it.[1]

How do we get through them? The times that knock the breath out; when even our strongest and bravest must confess with desolate eyes, "I do not know what to pray" (to paraphrase what Paul expresses in Rom. 8:26). How do we get through such times, when silences trump sentences? It is as if our words have no life jackets. They must stay, tread water in the shallows, and watch us from a distance. Words have no strength to venture with us into the heaving deeps that swallow us.

1   Charles Spurgeon, "The Fainting Hero," *MTP*, Vol. 55.

And many of us who believe in Jesus don't like to admit it, but we find no immunity here either. Many of us know what it is to lose hair, weight, appetite and the semblance of ourselves. Painful circumstances or a disposition of gloom within our chemistry can put on their muddy boots and stand thick, full weighted and heavy upon our tired chests. It is almost like anxiety tying rope around the ankles and hands of our breath. Tied to a chair, with the lights out, we sit swallowing in panic the dark air.

These kinds of circumstances and bodily chemistry can steal the gifts of divine love too, as if all of God's love letters and picture albums are burning up in a fire just outside the door, a fire which we are helpless to stop. We sit there, helpless in the dark of divine absence, tied to this chair, present only to ash and wheeze, while all we hold dear seems lost forever. We even wonder if we've brought this all on ourselves. It's our fault. God is against us. We've forfeited God's help.

Mentally, all of this, and its only Tuesday!

How do we get through?

Our Sense of Helplessness

One November morning, a preacher named Charles Spurgeon used his sermon to describe harmful helpers who like to tell the depressed, "Oh! You should not feel like this!" Or "Oh! You should not speak such words, nor think such thoughts."[2] Then, he offered a strong word of advocacy for sufferers of depression. "It is not easy to tell how another ought to feel and how another ought to act," he said.

---

2   Charles Spurgeon, "The Exaltation of Christ," Sermon 101, *NPSP* (November 2, 1856). http://www.spurgeon.org/sermons/0101.htm, accessed April 3, 2013.

We are different, each one of us; but I am sure there is one thing in which we are all brought to unite in times of deep sorrow, namely, in a sense of helplessness.[3]

We sense helplessness, yes, and also shame. Like other issues of mental health, we don't talk about depression. If we do, we either whisper as if the subject is scandalous or rebuke it as if it's a sin. No wonder many of us don't seek help; for when we do, those who try to help only add to the shame of it all.

How is it then that this preacher could stand up publicly in a congregation and talk so openly about depression? He was a megachurch pastor, one of the first ever. It was the 1800s. He was British, Victorian and Baptist. How was a guy like that talking so openly about a subject like this?

The answer is partially discovered in a catastrophic grief. Only two weeks prior to this early November sermon, when he talked about helplessness and he defended the depressed, he had preached to several thousand people in that exact spot. But as he did, a prankster yelled, "Fire!" The resulting panic left seven dead and twenty-eight seriously injured.

Charles (may I call him that?) was only twenty-two years old, embracing the tenth month of his young marriage. He and his wife were wading diaper deep into the first month of parenting their twin boys in a new house full of unpacked boxes. Now, with so many people dead, newspapers across London cruelly and mercilessly blamed him. The senseless tragedy and the public accusation nearly broke Charles' mind, not only in those early moments but also with lasting effects.

---

3   Charles Spurgeon, "The Exaltation of Christ," Sermon 101, *NPSP* (November 2, 1856). http://www.spurgeon.org/sermons/0101.htm, accessed April 3, 2013.

I start our conversation about depression with this November sermon, amid the public honesty of a pastor and a congregation. I do so because this sermon reveals what the pained man said the first time he returned to a pulpit following the hoax that killed. He begins – and I hope that you too might see how helpful this is – by publicly confessing his humanity.

> I almost regret this morning that I have ventured to occupy this pulpit, because I feel utterly unable to preach to you for your profit. I had thought that the quiet and repose of the last fortnight had removed the effects of that terrible catastrophe; but on coming back to the same spot again, and more especially, standing here to address you, I feel somewhat of those same painful emotions which well-nigh prostrated me before. You will therefore excuse me this morning ... I have been utterly unable to study ... Oh, Spirit of God, magnify thy strength in thy servant's weakness, and enable him to honour his Lord, even when his soul is cast down within him.[4]

The fact that such a prominent Christian pastor struggled with depression and talked so openly about it invites us to friendship with a fellow sufferer. As this pastor and preacher grappled with faith and doubt, suffering and hope, we gained a companion on the journey. In his story we can begin to find our own. What he found of Jesus in the darkness can serve as a light for our own darkness.

My Beloved's Anguish

There comes a time in most of our lives in which we no longer have the strength to lift ourselves out or to pretend

---

4   Charles Spurgeon, "The Exaltation of Christ," Sermon 101, *NPSP*.

ourselves strong. Sometimes our minds want to break because life stomped on us and God didn't stop it. Like a family who watches their loved one slip and fall onto the rocks on a mountainside vacation when all was supposed to be beautiful and fun; or like a parent whose child was mistreated or shot while at school. Charles and those who lost their loved ones that terrible day had to come to terms with suffering in a house of God while the word was preached and a prankster cackled.

Questions fill our lungs. We mentally wheeze. We go numb. When on vacation or at school or at church, *that* kind of thing is not supposed to happen *there*.

Even the knees of a Jesus-follower will buckle. Charles' wife, Susannah, said of Charles at that time, "My beloved's anguish was so deep and violent, that reason seemed to totter in her throne, and we sometimes feared that he would never preach again."[5]

Though it cannot be said for all of us or for every person that we have loved, it remains true that, in this cherished case, Charles Spurgeon did preach again. But sorrows of many kinds haunted and hounded him for the rest of his life. His depression came, not only from circumstances, or from questions about whether or not he was consecrated to God, but also from the chemistry of his body. God gave to us a preacher who knew firsthand what it felt like for his reason to totter, not just once, but many times during his life and ministry. And somehow this fellow sufferer named Charles and his dear wife Susannah (who also

---

5   Charles Ray, *The Life of Susannah Spurgeon*, in *Morning Devotions by Susannah Spurgeon: Free Grace and Dying Love* (Edinburgh: The Banner of Truth Trust, 2006), p. 166.

suffered physically most of her adult life) still made a go of it, insisting to each other and to their generation that the sorrowing have a Savior.

On that November morning, in weakness, Charles did what some of us are not yet able to do in our sorrows; he read the Bible. Perhaps it will comfort you to learn that for a while "the very sight of the Bible" made Charles cry.[6] Many of us know what this feels like. But this Scripture passage, Philippians 2:9-11, "had such a power of comfort upon [his] distressed spirit."

> And being found in human form, he [Jesus] humbled himself by becoming obedient to the point of death, even death on a cross. Therefore God has highly exalted him and bestowed on him the name that is above every name (Phil. 2:8-9).

From this Scripture, Charles set the larger story of his hope before us. The same Heavenly Father who picked up His son out of the muck, misery and mistreatment can do the same for us.

Finding Strength

You may or may not know what you think about that right now. But we know for sure, you and I, that more frequently than we want, our roads are often dirt and heat, all ants and flies. Sometimes our feet can't tap when the music plays.

We also know, don't we, that some of our friends exude impatience with us who must walk these roads of sorrow. Their ways are all jokes and pub, backslaps and slogans.

---

6   Charles Spurgeon, "Honey in the Mouth," *MTP,* Vol. 37 (Ages Digital Library, 1998), p. 485.

I don't pretend that a little book like this can mend such double-wounds or that the story of one person, like Charles Spurgeon, can bring comfort into your life.

Yet, I do know this. When our noses are rubbed red by tissue and our head hair falls out, have you noticed that we can still sometimes muster ourselves to welcome the child's drawing or the well-wisher's handwritten note? We can't take the philosopher's treatise or the theologian's lectures. The friend who motors on with sentences, too impatient for silences, must also wait to visit us on a later day. Sick inside, we simply cannot stomach a full meal. But a bit of cracker can help. A fragment of ice, a few syllables of a word timely chosen in friendship, can go a long way, sometimes, can't they?

And no one should think that life-giving nutrients are absent with such a seemingly sparse diet in the barren time. On the contrary, the sad-ridden and gracious-held in Jesus often testify to us regarding the surprising nourishment given with a few bits of daily bread. Day by day the strength finds them and carries them, though they know not how or when the carrying came.

I write this book with prayerful hope that its few bits will likewise nourish you in His carrying. I want to help you get through. So, rather than an exhaustive word or prosaic treatise on depression, I rather hope that you can receive it as it is intended; the handwritten note of one who wishes you well. Such notes of grace I too have sorely needed.

2

Depression and Our Circumstances

The mind can descend far lower than the body, for in it there are bottomless pits. The flesh can bear only a certain number of wounds and no more, but the soul can bleed in ten thousand ways, and die over and over again each hour.[1]

The umbrella was gray like the clouds. I held it above them as they knelt on mud covered with green tarp. They knelt there beneath the rain, next to the grave pit. They knelt there with the Bible open, reading, "I am the resurrection and the life." The pages were blotched by large wet drops, not so much from the rain as from their tears.

They cried too with loud voices. They shouted. Sometimes it was prayer they bellowed while I held the umbrella and the crowd stood gray and still. At other times it was as

---

1   Spurgeon, "Honey in the Mouth," *MTP,* Vol. 37, p. 485.

if deep groans burst through to catch and mangle the syllables, while she rocked her body back and forth, while he
knelt still but not quiet. We couldn't make out their sentences. But we didn't need to. The meaning was clear. A casket
this small, for a child this young, should not be.

Things in life can hurt us; circumstances we wouldn't
wish on anyone. They cause us to say with the Apostle
Paul, "our bodies had no rest, but we were afflicted at
every turn—fighting without and fear within" (2 Cor. 7:5).
Within a community of shrieking circumstances survivors
howl with rationality.

A voice was heard in Ramah,
    weeping and loud lamentation,
Rachel weeping for her children;
    she refused to be comforted, because they are no
more. (Matt. 2:18)

Even the beauty of wonder like childbirth can originate
words that can't get out of bed, words such as "post-partum."
"Who is there of our race that is quite free from sorrows?"
Charles asks us. "Search the whole earth through, and
everywhere the thorn and thistle will be found."[2]

"There is a time to weep," (Eccles. 3:4) no matter who
we are.

The Role of Painful Circumstances

Has a circumstance ever broken your heart? "There are
several forms of a broken heart,"[3] Charles tenderly reminds
us.

---

2   Charles Spurgeon, "The Man of Sorrows," *MTP*, Vol. 19 (Ages Digital
    Library, 1998), p. 155.

3   Charles Spurgeon, "Healing for the Wounded," *NPSP*, Sermon 53 (http://
    www.spurgeon.org/sermons/0053.htm), accessed 12/13/13.

- *Desertion*: Neglect or betrayal by a spouse, family member or friend.

- *Bereavement*: The ailment or death of one we love.

- *Penury*: Job loss, financial strain, poverty of basic needs.

- *Disappointment and Defeat*: Dreams unreached, goals blocked, tries that failed, foes that won.

- *Guilt*: regrets, pains we've caused others, sins against God.

More circumstances than these can traumatize us, here under this sun in this crime-ridden and tsunami world. The ancient sages teach us that being sad about such sad things is wise.

> It is better to go to the house of mourning
> > than to go to the house of feasting,
> for this is the end of all mankind,
> > and the living will lay it to heart. (Eccles. 7:2)

So, let's remind ourselves at the outset: In itself, sadness or "grief is God's gift to us. It's how we get through."[4] It is an act of faith and wisdom to be sad about sad things.

Depression a Symptom of Painful Circumstances

Sometimes sadness in response to painful circumstance takes a dark turn. It morphs into something other than itself. Grief doesn't end and the dark creature we call depression wakens from its lair.

---

4   Rick Warren quoted by Jaweed Kaleem, "Rick and Kay Warren Launch Mental Health Ministry at Saddleback Church After Son's Suicide," (March 31, 2014: Huffington Post): (http://www.huffingtonpost.com/2014/03/28/rick-warren-mental-health_n_5051129.html), accessed March 31, 2014.

"There are certain forms of disease," Charles observes, "which so affect the brain and the whole nervous system that depression is a melancholy symptom of the disease."[5]

> Quite involuntarily, unhappiness of mind, depression of spirit, and sorrow of heart will come upon you. You may be without any real reason for grief, and yet may become among the most unhappy of men because, for the time, your body has conquered your soul.[6]

Notice that Charles speaks of depression as if our choices are over-ruled. Depression comes "involuntarily" to us as if the thing has a will of its own. Notice also that an identifiable reason for the proportion of this grief does not exist. We exhibit unhappiness of mind whether the circumstances of our lives are good or bad.

Multiplied sadnesses can also take a dark turn toward depression. "Trial has succeeded trial," and blasted all of our hopes.[7] Trials become like waves on the sea rolling over us one after another. Such an "accumulation of aches, pains, weaknesses and sorrows" can take their toll on us.[8] Our boat begins to leak. Feverishly, while the waves roll in, we patch this hole and that one. The storm brews. Our boat rises and falls. Soon more holes appear than we have stamina to patch. The waters break over us. We held out as long as we could. The last wave proved too much. Our boat sank. In this case, is such

---

5   Charles Spurgeon, "The Fear of Death," *MTP*, Vol. 58 (Ages Digital Library, 198), p. 52.

6   Charles Spurgeon, "The Saddest Cry from the Cross," *MTP*, Vol. 48 (Ages Digital Library, 1998), p. 656.

7   Charles Spurgeon, "Sweet Stimulants for the Fainting Soul," *MTP*, Vol. 48 (Ages Digital Library, 1998), p. 575.

8   Charles Spurgeon, "Faintness and Refreshing," *MTP*, Vol. 54 (Ages Digital Library, 1998), p. 591.

depression actually "a grief out of proportion"? Or amid such suffering, is depression itself the warranted grief?

After all, for some of us, we've been unable to live in any other scene but the one that crushed us. We were brought so low that we never held up our heads again. It's like we will go from that time forth mourning to our graves.[9] Circumstance haunted us and went on. Depression came but never left. It haunts us still.

Perhaps among the hardest of our painful circumstances are those suffered in childhood. Depression seized its moment in our youth and something core to our temperament was altered permanently. We became like the sensitive plant that curls up its tendrils at a touch. Ever since, our lives have exhibited a constant shrinking from contact with other people. We no longer dare to face the world.[10] We assume the world stalks us, always to harm us.

How then do we tell the difference between the gift of sadness and the trauma of circumstantial depression? In his acclaimed book, *The Noonday Demon: An Atlas of Depression*, Andrew Solomon answers: "Grief is depression in proportion to circumstance" while "depression is grief out of proportion to circumstance."[11]

Let's pause for a moment and recognize how ugly ordinary grief in proportion to a circumstance can look. For example, what proportion of grief makes sense for a survivor of genocide? Or what of a mother whose son was murdered, or of a father whose daughter lost a long

---

9   Charles Spurgeon, "Weak Hands and Feeble Knees," Sermon 243 *NPSP* (http://www.spurgeon.org/sermons/0243.htm), accessed 3/6/14.

10   ibid.

11   Andrew Solomon, *The Noonday Demon: An Atlas of Depression* (New York: Scribner, 2003), p. 16.

fight with cancer and died young? How we define what is healthy and proportionate cannot be measured by our personal impatience or cultural decorum. The cruel thing itself must reveal the proportion of grief warranted.

No Cure for Sadness

In this light, contrary to what some people tell us, sadness is neither a sign of laziness nor a sin; neither negative thinking nor weakness. On the contrary, when we find ourselves impatient with sadness, we reveal our preference for folly, our resistance to wisdom, and our disregard for depth and proportion.

So, when we see others in pain, and we want to stop them from it, we must not underestimate what they have had to overcome in their lives. Depression calls for even more compassion and acceptance. They sin, yes. But we've all been sinned against too. If we had known the trials that have assaulted them, we too might discover a life more attended by frightful glooms and miserable stares within our memories than we want.

Memory after all is a powerful thing. It can both bless us and haunt us. Some of us are memory-haunted. Circumstance left its stain. Such persons need mercy not scolding. After all, on this side of heaven, "There is no cure for sadness"[12] or depression. No saint or hero is immune. Room to cry loudly or long remains necessary, warranted, and nobly human.

So as we head into our next chapter, let's hold the soaked umbrella together by the graveside and establish this important truth. In this fallen world, sadness is an act of sanity, our tears the testimony of the sane.

---

12   Susanna Kaysen, "One Cheer for Melancholy," in *Unholy Ghost: Writers on Depression* (New York: Perennial, 2002), p. 41.

What Depression Originating from Circumstances Teaches Us

1. Christian faith on earth is neither an escape nor heaven. Charles speaks of certain Christians who, from their position of health and wealth, suggest that perfection, ease and immunity from human troubles describe what faithfulness to Jesus produces. Charles counters this notion and describes instead "the tried people of God" who "do not often ride upon these high horses." The sheer number of their anxieties and cares forces them into a life which must frequently cry out to God and which exposes their being only mortal.[13]

2. We do not equate spiritual blessing with circumstantial ease. "Certain of my brethren are frequently in trouble. Their whole life is a floundering out of one slough of despond into another. You have had many losses in business—nothing but losses perhaps; you have had many crosses, disappointments, bereavements; nothing prospers with you ... it is no sign, beloved, that you are not a child of God ... remember that none of your trials can prove you to be a lost man."[14]

3. We who've not suffered depression from circumstances must learn the pastoral care of those who have. When a person "has been through a similar experience" of depression, "he uses another tone of voice altogether. He knows that, even if it is nonsense to the strong, it is not so to the weak, and he so adapts his remarks so that he cheers"

---

13   Charles Spurgeon, "Night and Jesus Not There!" *MTP*, Vol. 51 (Ages Digital Library, 1998), p. 457.

14   Charles Spurgeon, "The Believer Sinking in the Mire," *MTP*, vol. 11 (Ages Digital Library, 1998), p. 361.

the sufferer "where the other only inflicts additional pain. Broken hearted one, Jesus Christ knows all your troubles, for similar troubles were his portion" too.[15]

---

15 Charles Spurgeon, "Binding Up Broken Hearts," *MTP*, Vol. 54 (Ages Digital Library, 1998), p. 491.

3

The Disease of Melancholy

I would not blame all those who are much given to fear, for in some it is rather their disease than their sin, and more their misfortune than their fault.[1]

Sometimes depression doesn't stem from painful circumstances. According to Charles, "Some persons are constitutionally sad."[2] Sometimes we are marked by melancholy from the moment of our birth.[3]

---

1   Charles Spurgeon, "Away with Fear," *MTP*, Vol. 16 (http://www. spurgeongems.org/vols16-18/chs930.pdf), 16. Accessed March 9, 2014

2   Charles Spurgeon, "Joy, Joy, Forever!," *MTP*, Vol. 36 (Ages Digital Library, 1998), p. 373.

3   Charles Spurgeon, "Joyful Transformations," *MTP, The Spurgeon Archive* (http://www.spurgeon.org/joyful.htm), accessed 12/13/13.

Marked From Birth

What difference does this melancholy birthmark make in a person's life? Answering this question can help us who suffer begin to know ourselves better and those who love us to gain understanding.

To begin, our imagination can possess a darker edge. As Charles observed, "All our birds are owls or ravens."[4] When "one is born with a melancholy temperament, he sees a tempest brewing even in the calm."[5]

We are also prone to exaggerated fears. "Desponding people," according to Charles, "can find reason for fear where no fear is."[6]

This makes it harder for us to find relief or assurance of safety. If things are calm, we look for what harm awaits us. If things go wrong, we assume that the worst is yet to come. We imagine doom futures, and though none of the bad things we imagine have happened to us, we "convert our suspicions into realities and torture" ourselves with them in our own imaginations.[7]

So, unlike others whose doubts and fears subside, our "constitutional temperament is such that it keeps on doubting."[8] Worries and anxieties of many kinds assail us. "On the very slightest turn of circumstances we begin to fret."[9] Everybody frets and worries, of course. But the disease intensifies it. We worry more. We fear more.

---

4   Charles Spurgeon, "First Things First," *MTP*, Vol. 31 (Ages Digital Library, 1998), p. 712.

5   Charles Spurgeon, "Divine Sovereignty," *NPSP*, Sermon 77, *The Spurgeon Archive* (http://www.spurgeon.org/sermons/0077.htm), accessed 12/13/13.

6   Charles Spurgeon, "Away with Fear," *MTP*, Vol. 16 (Ages Digital Library, 1998), p. 338.

7   ibid.

8   Charles Spurgeon, "A Prayer for the Church Militant," *MTP*, Vol. 13, Sermon 768 (Ages Digital Library).

9   Charles Spurgeon, "The Yoke Removed and the Lord Revealed," *MTP*, Vol. 25 (Ages Digital Library, 1998), p. 183.

Sometimes our ordinary responsibilities, therefore, make us anxious and overwhelmed. Performance anxiety undoes us. Little things feel giant. "A man may feel that he ought to do so well that, for that very reason, he may not do as well as he might. An overwhelming feeling of responsibility may breed paralysis."[10] Unless we can do it perfectly we won't try it at all.

Often then, feeling unable to do what our responsibilities demand, we are harassed by accusing and condemning thoughts regarding our every mistake and blunder, both real and imagined. We can finally go numb. It is as if we shut down and feel so much that we feel nothing at all.

Does this resonate with your experience? Depression is like a darkness that drapes over us wherever we go. "When people are in the dark they are afraid of anything, everything!"[11] So, when we feel constantly in the dark mentally, we quiver and tremble at what lurks around the corner.

Not always of course. Depression has its seasons of "remission". We are not harassed each and every moment. Sometimes rest comes. The cellar doors open and we walk quite happily into the sunshine glad and at ease. But the "black crow"[12] wants and waits to swoop down upon us again and sometimes he does.

Biological marks from birth like this can even produce certain types of "physical disorder," according to Charles. A melancholy "imagination" might increase and intensify what ails us, but nonetheless "depression of spirit" stems from "a real disease, it is not imaginary."[13] These biological

---

10 Charles Spurgeon, *The Greatest Fight in the World* (Ages Digital Library, 1998), p. 3.

11 Charles Spurgeon, "How to Meet the Doctrine of Election," *MTP*, Vol. 30 (Ages Digital Library, 1998), p. 609.

12 Kenyon, "Having it Out With Melancholy," p. 233.

13 Charles Spurgeon, "The Cause and Cure of a Wounded Spirit," *MTP*, Vol. 42 (Ages Digital Library, 1998), p. 786.

cases, Charles says plainly, require "the business of the physician" more than of the pastor or theologian.[14] Pastors and Christians need medical professionals on their pastoral care team.

The Body Alters Our Moods

By identifying some forms of depression with disease,[15] Charles imitates a book in his library written by Timothy Rogers entitled *Trouble of Mind, and the Disease of Melancholy*. Rogers defined melancholy in a manner typical of the times, referring to how it alters us and hardens us against joy.[16] Depression is a joy thief.

This burglar of joy also likes to plunder our sense of God. "There are some true souls whom God loves," Charles observes, "who yet do not often enjoy a sunshiny day; they are very dark as to their hope and their joy, and some of them have perhaps, for months, lost the light of God's countenance."[17]

Now, what I'm about to write needs our attention. Depression can so vandalize our joy and our sense of God that no promise of His can comfort us in the moment, no matter how true or kindly spoken. At its worst, "Everything in the world looks dark." Even God's mercies frighten us "and rise like hideous portents of evil" before our mind's eye.[18]

---

14   Spurgeon, "Cause and Cure of a Wounded Spirit," p. 786.

15   Charles Spurgeon, "Bells for the Horses," in *Sword and Trowel* (http://www.spurgeon.org/s_and_t/bells.htm), accessed 12/13/13.

16   Timothy Rogers, (1660-1729) *"Trouble of Mind, and the Disease of Melancholy,"* Quoted in Charles Spurgeon, *The Treasury of David*, Psalm 107, Explanatory Notes and Quaint Sayings (http://www.spurgeon.org/treasury/ps107.htm), accessed 12/13/13.

17   Spurgeon, "Means for Restoring the Banished," p. 645.

18   Charles Spurgeon, "The Garden of the Soul," *MTP*, Vol. 12 (Ages Digital Library, 1998), p. 370.

Let's pause for a moment here to highlight three important helps.

1. *As a sufferer or caregiver, we must take into account the body's contribution to depression.* On this point, Charles reminds us of basic Christian theology. "Man is a double being: he is composed of body and soul, and each of the portions of man may receive injury and hurt."[19]

2. *Depression is not a sin.* Though sins can result from it and temptations intensify because of it, depression itself is not a sin. "We may get depressed in spirit; we may be nervous, fearful, timid; we may almost come to the borders of despair," and this "apart from sin."[20] Sometimes what threatens God's absence in our life is not our hard heart but a physiological prankster.

3. *Depression is not unique to us.* After citing historical examples such as Martin Luther, Isaac Newton, and William Cowper, then Biblical examples such as Job, King David, Elijah or our Lord Jesus, Charles will inevitably say: "You are not the first child of God who has been depressed or troubled." Even "among the noblest of men and women who ever lived, there has been much of this kind of thing ... Do not, therefore, think that you are quite alone in your sorrow." Even though you may "go to bed in the dark," you will "wake up in the eternal daylight."[21]

---

19   Charles Spurgeon, "Healing for the Wounded," *NPSP*, Sermon 53 in *The Spurgeon Archive* http://www.spurgeon.org/sermons/0053.htm, accessed 12/13/13.

20   Charles Spurgeon, "Our Youth Renewed," *MTP*, Vol. 60 (Ages Digital Library, 1998), p. 462.

21   Charles Spurgeon, "The Cause and Cure of a Wounded Spirit," *MTP*, Vol. 42 (Ages Digital Library, 1998), pp. 791-792.

Grace Relieves But Does Not Always Cure Depression
But isn't following Jesus supposed to change all of this? Isn't Jesus supposed to heal our diseases? Many of us feel that if we were more true to Jesus we wouldn't struggle this way. Others actually tell us earnestly that our salvation in Jesus is threatened and put into question.

But just as a man with asthma or a woman born mute will likely remain this way even though they love Jesus, so our mental disorders and melancholy inclinations often remain with us too. Conversion to Jesus isn't heaven, but its foretaste. This side of heaven, grace secures us but doesn't cure us. "There are lines of weakness in the creature which even grace does not efface."[22] Though substantial healing can come, Charles reminds us that often it waits till heaven to complete its full work.

> We do not profess that the religion of Christ will so thoroughly change a man as to take away from him all his natural tendencies; it will give the despairing something that will alleviate that despondency, but as long as that is caused by a low state of body, or a diseased mind, we do not profess that the religion of Christ will totally remove it. No, rather, we do see every day that amongst the best of God's servants, there are those who are always doubting, always looking to the dark side of every providence, who look at the threatening more than at the promise, who are ready to write bitter things against themselves ...[23]

Therefore we sufferers of depression in Christ may grow terribly weak, even in faith, but we are not lost to God. Contrary to those who tell us that we do not have enough faith or that we are condemned because of our inability to

---

22 Charles Spurgeon, "Faintness and Refreshing," in *the Metropolitan Tabernacle Pulpit*, Vol. 54 (Ages Digital Library, 1998), p. 590.

23 Charles Spurgeon, "Weak Hands and Feeble Knees," *NPSP*, Sermon 243 in *The Spurgeon Archive* (http://www.spurgeon.org/sermons/0243.htm), accessed 12/13/13.

smile more, "Depression of spirit is no index of declining grace."[24] It is Christ and not the absence of depression that saves us. So, we declare this truth. Our sense of God's absence does not mean that He is so. Though our bodily gloom allows us no feeling of His tender touch, He holds on to us still. Our feelings of Him do not save us. He does.

Our hope therefore, does not reside in our ability to preserve a good mood but in His ability to bear us up. Jesus will never abandon us with our downcast heart. Take comfort from how Charles puts it.

> Perhaps you are not well, or you have had an illness that has tolled much upon your nervous system, and you are depressed; and therefore it is that you think that grace is leaving you, but it will not. Your spiritual life does not depend upon nature, else it might expire; it depends upon grace, and grace will never cease to shine till it lights you into glory.[25]

We know that though every cloud darkens with storm brew, the sun yet shines. We who've flown in airplanes can attest to this truth.

We also know that though we toss and turn in restless and sickly sleep, our loved one holds our hand and wipes the sweat from our head in the night deeps, though we know it not. So it is with God, while our bodies sometimes make a wreck of our moods and cast doubts upon our faith, He holds us secure, though we know it not, and our fit continues to rage.

Remember, depression is a "misfortune not a fault," Charles reminded us in the opening quote of this chapter; a kind of struggle that does not warrant our condemnation.

---

24   Charles Spurgeon, "Sweet Stimulants for the Fainting Soul," in *The Metropolitan Tabernacle Faith*, Vol. 48 (Ages Digital Library, 1998), p. 575.

25   Charles Spurgeon, "Smoking Flax," *MTP*, Vol. 31 (Ages Digital Library, 1998), p. 224.

What does this mean? In contrast to those who would tell you to get stronger and plead your strengths with God, Charles counters and tells us the opposite: "Let your weakness plead with God through Jesus Christ."[26] His mercies are large enough, deep enough, wide enough, high enough to hold secure what you cannot. Grace for your need rises to the occasion (Heb. 4:12). Your hope is not your health but His ability to be the strength you need.

God Does Not Laugh At Our Depression
As I conclude this chapter, I recognize that I've begun to talk explicitly about God. Many of us might find this very hard to take. God-talk has not been kind and our miseries have been too real for trite or mean religious people to handle. You are right about this and I hope that each chapter from here on will prove useful to you as it relates to God and your depression.

For the moment though, it might interest you to know that Charles, in his depression, somehow saw God as compassionate toward him and toward all of us who suffer in this way. He distinguished those who mocked him from God Himself. Here is what he said:

> Some of you may be in great distress of mind, a distress out of which no fellow-creature can deliver you. You are poor nervous people at whom others often laugh. I can assure you that God will not laugh at you; he knows all about that sad complaint of yours, so I urge you to go to him, for the experience of many of us has taught us that, "the Lord is gracious and full of compassion."[27]

---

26   Charles Spurgeon, "The Frail Leaf," *MTP*, Vol. 57 (Ages Digital Library, 1998), p. 595.

27   Charles Spurgeon, "Remembering God's Works," *MTP*, Vol. 49 (Ages Digital Library, 1998), p. 591.

4

Spiritual Depression

*Spiritual sorrows are the worst of mental
miseries.*[1]

In his poem "The Castaway" William Cowper wrote of
a shipwrecked man who died at sea. Nearing the end of
the poem, he tells us why he meditates on the man who
sank beneath the waves.

> But misery still delights to trace
> Its semblance in another's case.

---

1   Charles Spurgeon, "Lama Sabachthani?" *MTP*, Vol. 36 (Ages Digital
     Library, 1998), p. 168.

After telling us this; that the miserable find comfort in the shared stories of other miserable ones, Cowper uses the man who drowned at sea as a metaphor to describe his own depression.

No voice divine the storm allayed,
No light propitious shone;
When, snatched from all effectual aid,
We perished, each alone:
But I beneath a rougher sea,
And whelmed in deeper gulfs than he.[2]

Cowper describes himself as left alone by God. No aid comes; only the overwhelming deeps. Yet, the same man who wrote this poem also wrote hymns of faith that to this day bless Christian congregations.

Ye fearful saints, fresh courage take;
The clouds ye so much dread
Are big with mercy and shall break
In blessings on your head.

Judge not the Lord by feeble sense,
But trust Him for His grace;
Behind a frowning providence
He hides a smiling face.[3]

Religious Melancholy

In Charles' generation, the *Manual of Psychological Medicine* identified what it termed "religious melancholia". Associated mostly with insanity, this form of depression

---

2   William Cowper, "The Castaway," (http://www.poets.org/poetsorg/poem/castaway), accessed May 5, 2014.

3   William Cowper, "God Moves in a Mysterious Way," *Olney Hymns* (http://www.cyberhymnal.org/bio/c/o/w/cowper_w.htm), accessed May 5, 2014.

afflicts persons at every moment with conscious and unstoppable terrors of God's displeasure. Or, those who suffered this kind of depression used extreme acts of religious devotion in ways that harmed themselves or others. Cowper often experienced the former, enduring the hellish thought that the God whom he loved had grace for others but not for him.

The *Manual* cites how well-meaning but errant preachers contribute to the spiritual agony of depression:

> It is hardly necessary to say that Christianity undistorted, and preached in its just proportions, is calculated to prevent, not cause, insanity. The exciting cause of religious melancholia is sometimes to be traced to fiery denunciations of a well-meaning but injudicious preacher.[4]

Sometimes preachers and Christian talkers forget that those who listen to them live with various circumstantial and biological ailments and trials. They forget the care a shepherd would provide should a member of the flock suffer these kinds of afflictions. For Cowper, a dear and kind gift of a pastor was given him. John Newton, the writer of *Amazing Grace*, was Cowper's pastor and friend.

In our day, sentiments similar to these can remain. Religion offers both a challenge and a help to those who suffer mental disorders. This challenge surfaces when preachers assume that depression is always and only a sin. They pour gasoline on the fire and wonder why it rages rather than calms those they try to help. At the same time, studies today confirm that those with mental

---

4   *Manual of Psychological Medicine*, p. 179.

health challenges simply do much better if they are part of a religious community.[5]

In this tug of war with God and depression, Charles recognized a spiritual reality to depression. He felt that depression itself has circumstantial, biological and spiritual contributors and challenges. But he also believed that the spiritual side of things could originate its own kind of depression. In other words, someone with biological depression will have spiritual realities to contend with. But a person might suffer from spiritual depression even though they've had no circumstantial or biological depression to speak of.

John Bunyan's famed story, *Pilgrim's Progress*, gave language to Charles as he tried to help those who suffered (as well as describe what could assail him as well). In Bunyan's story, the main character named Christian falls into the Slough of Despond, is later captured by Giant Despair, and then beaten mercilessly in Doubting Castle. Despondency, despair and doubt join together to create spiritual miseries in our lives.

The Symptoms of Spiritual Depression

What is this spiritual melancholy? At its core, spiritual depression concerns real or imagined desertions by God. We feel in our senses that He is angry with us, or we have done something to forfeit His love, or He has toyed with us and left us on a whim. Either way, He exists for others, but not for us. He punishes us with silent treatment. He laughs at our pain when He gossips to others about us.

---

5   Lauren Cahoon, "Will God Get You Out of Your Depression?" (ABC News, March 19, 2008) http://abcnews.go.com/Health/MindMoodNews/story?id=4454786, accessed May 4, 2014.

The irony of desertion is that God's absence feels overwhelmingly close to us. We stare the void in the face. According to Charles, when a person knows that God is with them, he or she "may bear great depression of spirit." "But if we believe God has left us in our miseries and hardships, there is a torment within the breast which I can only liken," Charles says, "to the prelude of hell." Persons can "bare a bleeding body, and even a wounded spirit; but a soul conscious of desertion by God is beyond conception unendurable."[6]

Various horrible symptoms rise from desertion. To begin, we can magnify every weakness, limit, sin and imperfection within us. We terribly doubt whether we "are Christians at all," and become "tormented with the fear" that we are frauds living sham lives.[7]

We can become fixated and "sore distressed with questions" we cannot answer, "enigmas" we cannot solve, and knots of difficulty we cannot untie. We turn to all or nothings. Because we do not know *everything* we believe we cannot know *anything*. We refuse comfort.

We may then view the Bible itself in extremes. It becomes either a book of whips gleeful to strike us by its every word with our impending doom. Or in reverse, it becomes a dry word, uninteresting, irrelevant toward us. If the Bible happily whips and dooms us we writhe and moan for the absent God to deliver us. If the scriptures have dried up, we become numb and indifferent. Dreadful apathy sets in. "We want to feel, but cannot feel."[8]

---

6   Charles Spurgeon, "Lama Sabachthani?," *MTP*, Vol. 36 (Ages Digital Library, 1998), p. 168.

7   Charles Spurgeon, "A Call to the Depressed," *MTP*, Vol. 60 (Ages Digital Library, 1998), p. 536.

8   ibid.

"Spiritual insomnia" may toss and turn us. Restless, we strive, agonize, fret and worry. We work all the harder, never able to do enough, conscious only that our results are too small, and that God remains constantly displeased. We never measure up and we spend our days fretting and anxious that God will walk away shaking His head at us unless we get it all right or good enough.[9]

Eventually we wear out or wear thin. "The enjoyment of service evaporates, the fretfulness which pines over details spoils the whole, and the worker becomes a mere drudge and scullion."[10] These imagined withdrawals of God from us can torture the mind.

Have you ever experienced this?

But the most terrible of these spiritual symptoms Charles calls "heaviness of spirit." In opposite to what I've just described, this kind of distance from God is real and not imagined. We see the true horror of our sin, we feel ourselves worthy of legitimate judgment and beyond all hope or worthiness of forgiveness. But we see no remedy and no hope for recovery.

From his own experience, Charles urges us that if we had suffered "half an hour" of this kind of true conviction of actual sin we would have more compassion on those who suffer in this way. "To be impaled upon your own sins, pilloried by your own conscience, shot at by your own judgment as with barbed arrows—this is anguish and torment." "Next to the torment of hell," the bitterness of true remorse and despair reveals the worst of our sorrows—worse even than death itself.[11]

---

9   Charles Spurgeon, "Faint, But Not Fainthearted," *MTP*, Vol. 40 (Ages Digital Library, 1998), p. 20.

10   Charles Spurgeon, "Martha and Mary," *MTP*, Vol. 16 (Ages Digital Library, 1998), p. 297.

11   ibid.

In all of these symptoms we misjudge our hope. We imagine ourselves with no remedy for forgiveness or reconciliation, as if God did not so love the world and did not give His own Son.

Making matters worse is that others commonly think we are "over the top" and "too often condemn[s] and even ridicule[s] him who is sad of soul."[12] So, not only do we feel deserted by God but we also feel shamed and deserted by those who talk about God. We therefore suffer a double sense of abandonment and feel no hope for healing. No Savior from sin, no sympathy for the sorrowing—we reason in tortures.

The Spiritual Vulnerability of the Melancholy

At this point, we want to remind ourselves that suffering one form of depression makes the addition of others harder to bear. For example, if someone doesn't like us, this rejection looms larger "in times of depression". What would have stung us for a day now turns into a desire to get away from people.[13]

Likewise, if someone struggles already with biological or circumstantial depression, they are more vulnerable to spiritual sorrows.[14] It is hard enough to get through the day without adding the displeasure of God to the trauma that already trounces us.

As an example, Charles tells us personally how his own ongoing struggle with doubts is made harder due to

12 Charles Spurgeon, "The Garment of Praise," *MTP*, Vol. 59 (Ages Digital Library, 1998), p. 226.

13 Spurgeon, *Autobiography*, Chapter 32, p. 400.

14 Charles Spurgeon, "Hope in Hopeless Cases," *MTP*, Vol. 14 (Ages Digital Library, 1998), p. 492.

depression. It is very hard to stand day by day and say, "No, I cannot doubt my God," when we are already assaulted by that "perpetual stabbing, and cutting, and hacking" at our faith. It is not so easy to endure.[15]

Two helps come to mind here.

1. *Remember to account for one's context of life.* Slow your judgment down. "When you see men faint, do not blame them. Perhaps, by their faintness, they have proved of what stuff they are made. They have done as much as flesh and blood can do, and therefore they are faint."[16] Who knows what multiplied sorrows they've endured?

2. *Remember, it has required more faith for some to do less than you.* Some "need not be afraid of the Slough of Despond, for they carry a slough within their own hearts, and are never out of it, or it is never out of them." There is "much to admire" in the perseverance required of these dear ones and in the Savior who cares for them. Our hearts need compassion. "Trembling fellow pilgrims, we would play the harp for you, that, if possible you may forget your fears awhile; and if you cannot altogether rise superior to your glooms, yet may you, for this hour at least, take unto yourselves the wings of eagles and mount above the mists of doubt."[17]

Now let's look at one more important contributor to depression in general and spiritual depression in particular. Charles believed in an actual devil. This creature does not

---

15 Charles Spurgeon, "The Roaring Lion," *MTP*, Vol. 7 (Ages Digital Library, 1998), p. 1040.

16 Spurgeon, "Faint; But Not Fainthearted," p. 19.

17 Charles Spurgeon, "The Sweet Harp of Consolation," *MTP*, Vol. 13 (Ages Digital Library, 1998), p. 476.

originate or cause depression. But like a lion drawn to the weakened zebra in the herd, this evil creature derives peculiar pleasure from devouring those who are lame, sick, or debilitated.

In other words, "The great enemy makes a dead set at anxious souls."[18] He delights in taking sorrows and making more of them. Like Giant Despair, Satan "lashes his poor slave with excess of malice, if by any means he may utterly destroy his victim before the deliverer arrives."[19] Accusation, condemnation, and cruel whispers pile upon the already wheezing sufferer. If we are not careful, we imitate this accusing cruel one in our attempts to help or rouse ourselves or our depressed friends.

For, when depression assails us, with Cowper we tell ourselves that we are not a true child of God. We have no hope, our sins have found us out, our questions are too numerous, our future is doomed, our present worthy only of apathy, and our forgiveness impossible. This ancient evil creature smiles and says, "Yes, yes, you are right. Oh, but it is worse than you thought. All is lost. You are abandoned and rightly so. You are forfeit. Stay down. You are out of reach. It is too late for you. Sinner! They are better off without you. You deserve to die."

Feed Not This Frenzy of the Soul![20]
It is here, when dealing with spiritual depression, that Charles takes a marked turn in his usually gentle approach

---

18 Charles Spurgeon, "Loving Advice for Anxious Seekers," *MTP*, Vol. 13 (Ages Digital Library, 1998), p. 107.

19 Spurgeon, "Hope in Hopeless Cases," p. 492.

20 Charles Spurgeon, "New Uses for Old Trophies," *MTP*, Vol. 17 (Ages Digital Library, 1998), p. 73.

as a caregiver and sufferer. Many circumstantial, biological and spiritual pains outlast our abilities to control them or understand them. But, when we face this ancient foe, the devil, there remains only one thing we can and must do. "Fight!"

> The soul is broken in pieces, lanced, pricked with knives, dissolved, racked, pained. It knows not how to exist when it gives way to fear. Up, Christian! You are of a sorrowful countenance; up and chase your fears. Why would you be ever groaning in your dungeon? Why should Giant Despair forever beat you with his Crabtree cudgel? Up! Drive him away![21]

How? In essence, we use the phrase, "you might be right, but Jesus."

- You might be right, things are worse than I thought, but Jesus!

- You might be right, all is lost, but Jesus!

- You might be right, I am abandoned, but Jesus!

- You might be right, I am forfeit, but Jesus!

- You might be right, I should stay down, but Jesus!

- You might be right, it would be too late for me, but Jesus!

- You might be right, I am out of reach, but Jesus!

- You might be right, I am a sinner, but Jesus!

- You might be right, they might be better off without me, but Jesus!

- You might be right, I could deserve to die, but Jesus!

---

21 Charles Spurgeon, "Fear Not," *NPSP*, Vol. 3 (Ages Digital Library, 1998), p. 651.

We plead not ourselves, but the promises of Jesus; not our strengths but His; our weaknesses yes, but His mercies. Our way of fighting is to hide behind Jesus who fights for us. Our hope is not the absence of our regret, or misery or doubt or lament, but the presence of Jesus. "Doubting Castle may be very strong, but he who comes to fight with Giant Despair is stronger still!"[22]

In pleading Jesus we embrace what Charles called "a blessed kind of despair" which is the work of God Himself on our behalf.

> —a despair of self salvation, a despair of washing away your own sin, despair of obtaining any merit of your own by which you can become acceptable in the sight of God ... That is a blessed kind of despair; but in reference of any other sort of despair ... I cannot say anything that is good.[23]

Just as William Cowper found a gift of grace in his friend and pastor, John Newton, so we too need such gifts. Whether we feel banished by God because of sin, or because of despondency, either way "how graciously our heavenly Father sends to his afflicted," not only Himself, but also "words of good cheer by persons who have passed through similar experiences."[24]

Spurgeon's Three Tough Words
Due to the severity of misery caused by spiritual depression, Charles becomes a strong advocate and tough caregiver in three circumstances.

---

22 Charles Spurgeon, "Christ Looseth From Infirmities," *MTP*, Vol. 56 (Ages Digital Library, 1998), p. 282.

23 Charles Spurgeon, "A Discourse for the Despairing," *MTP*, Sermon 2379 (http://www.spurgeongems.org/vols40-42/chs2379.pdf), accessed 3/19/14.

24 Charles Spurgeon, "Means for Restoring the Banished," *MTP*, Vol. 16 (Ages Digital Library, 998), p. 645.

First, Charles defends sufferers by getting tough with preachers (including himself) who tell poor despondent ones that Jesus will not come to them unless they suffer enough or get themselves better enough to be worthy. Critical of himself, of John Bunyan,[25] and other preachers, Charles says plainly. "If, when I was a youth, I had heard the gospel of Christ preached as plainly as I have preached it to you, I feel certain that I should never have been in the bog so long as I was."[26] Consequently, Charles in his sermons regularly points sufferers of Doubting Castles and Sloughs of Despond to an immediate encounter of grace with the living Jesus.[27]

Second, Charles defends sufferers by getting tough with the intentionally chosen melancholy of the religious who haunt themselves on purpose with the dreaded notion that somebody somewhere might be happy.[28] Such persons take it upon themselves to shush the joy out of people in the name of God. This kind of religion makes a mockery of the pain suffered in true depression and sorrows. It also cruelly blocks needy sufferers from the relieving smiles of a gracious God by falsely condemning any brightness or joy as unholy or unrighteous.

Third, Charles on *rare occasion* will risk offending sufferers of other kinds of depression in order to reach the spiritual sufferer who refuses to fight. In this light, I caution

---

25 In multiple sermons, Spurgeon corrects what he believes was John Bunyan's mistake, to require Christian go through a slough of Despond before he could reach the wicket gate. See, "Prompt Obedience," *MTP*, Vol. 58 (Ages Digital Library, 1998), p. 414.

26 Charles Spurgeon, "The Free Agency of Christ," *MTP*, Vol. 48 (Ages Digital Library, 1998).

27 See for example Charles Spurgeon, "The Believer Sinking in the Mire," *MTP*, Vol. 11 (Ages Digital Library, 1998), 360; "Prisoners of Hope," *MTP*, Vol. 49 (Ages Digital Library, 1998), 431; "Soul Satisfaction," *MTP*, Vol. 55 (Ages Digital Library, 1998), p. 192.

28 Shenk, *Lincoln's Melancholy*, p. 87.

anyone before reading his sermon "A Call to the Depressed" to recognize this particular motive and focus. Otherwise, Charles' tone and words will likely prove harsh and unhelpful.

Charles likens this particular sermon to a severe surgery for a dire moment. He seems also to recognize the edge that he walks with this sermon. "Perhaps you may think it is rather hampering than helping you," he admits halfway through, "and tends more to depress than to deliver you."[29] But he continues with language that is not his norm: "I would say anything, however sharp, if it might but wake you out of your lethargy."

Yet, as the sermon goes on, sensing and perhaps regretting this sharpness within his tone, he begins to back off from it. "Methinks there is a better way than this," he says. Then, in the last quarter of the sermon, he recovers his usual gospel hope and begins to talk about his own suffering as a shared experience in need of grace. He concludes by reminding those who listen: "Look out for those who are in the same state as you have been in, and be very tender over them. As you know their case" by experience "and have traversed that howling desert" too.[30]

Perhaps in this sermon, we see Charles the human being trying imperfectly to administer help to sorrows not easily diagnosed. In his earnest and fragile attempts to help, we see our own.

Now What?
In our conversation together, what we've learned thus far is this. If "scientific and spiritual schools of thought" are both tempted to address depression by holding "onto

---

29   Charles Spurgeon, "A Call to the Depressed," *MTP*, Vol. 60 (Ages Digital Library, 1998), p. 540.

30   ibid., p. 542.

one explanation at the expense of the other,"[31] Charles has invited us to resist this temptation.

The pastor, religious counselor, or friend must learn to account for the medical, psychological and behavioral realities of depression. Conversely, the medical, therapeutic, psychological or behavioral caregiver mustn't dismiss the contribution of spiritual realities to circumstantial and biological depression.

We might summarize these categories as circumstance, chemistry and spirit. They each help us begin to understand depression and its kinds. The poet who suffered from depression gives us a hymn. His prayer can become our own.

> Heal us, Emmanuel, here we are
> We wait to feel Thy touch;
> Deep wounded souls to Thee repair,
> And Savior, we are such ...
>
> Remember him who once applied
> With trembling for relief;
> "Lord, I believe," with tears he cried;
> "O help my unbelief!"
>
> She, too, who touched Thee in the press
> And healing virtue stole,
> Was answered, "Daughter, go in peace;
> Thy faith has made thee whole."
>
> Like her, with hopes and fears we come
> To touch Thee if we may;
> O send us not despairing home;
> Send none unhealed away.[32]

---

31 Richard Winter, *Roots of Sorrow: Reflections on Depression and Hope* (Eugene, Oregon: Wipf & Stock Publishers, 2000), p. 34.

32 William Cowper, "Heal Us, Emmanuel," *Olney Hymns* (http://www.cyberhymnal.org/htm/h/e/healusem.htm), accessed May 5, 2014.

Part Two:

Learning How to Help those Who Suffer Depression

5

Diagnosis Doesn't Cure

"Especially judge not the sons and daughters of sorrow. Allow no ungenerous suspicions of the afflicted, the poor, and the despondent. Do not hastily say they ought to be more brave, and exhibit a greater faith. Ask not – 'why are they so nervous, and so absurdly fearful?' No ... I beseech you, remember that you understand not your fellow man."[1]

Some things, we never get over. We get through them or on with them, but not over them.

Twenty-five years after the hoax that killed, when someone yelled, "fire!" and many died, Charles was about to address a large audience during a session of the Baptist Union. He was older now, middle aged, a seasoned pastor and well known. All seats were taken and hundreds were

---

1   Charles Spurgeon, "Man Unknown to Man," *MTP*, Vol. 34, Sermon 2079 (http://www.spurgeongems.org/vols34-36/chs2079.pdf), accessed 12/14/13.

pressing in. Charles walked onto the platform and became "entirely unmanned ... leaning his head on his hand." Why?

This circumstance so vividly recalled the terrible scene at the Surrey Music Hall, that he felt quite unable to preach. But he did preach, and preach well, though he could not entirely recover the agitation of his nervous system.[2]

Charles experienced what we today might call a "flashback". A moment in time perfectly harmless that triggers memory of a previous moment that was full of harm. The one looks like the other and sets off a trauma response in our bodies and minds. Even the grace to preach well did not "entirely recover the agitation of his nervous system." Twenty-five years had passed and Charles still suffered in the present what traumatized him in the past. Twenty-five years ...

Diagnosing our circumstantial, biological and spiritual depressions offers aid. But diagnosis doesn't end the challenge for us.

Ungenerous Suspicions Still Remain

Because of this slowness or absence of cure, sufferers of depression must daily withstand voices of condemnation. After all, "Shouldn't you be over it by now?"

Condemnation comes from what Charles calls the "ungenerous suspicions" which many harbor toward those in depression. In the eyes of many people, including Christian people, depression signifies cowardice, faithlessness or a bad attitude. Such people tell God in prayer and their friends in person that the sufferer of depression is probably faking it or soft or unspiritual. To our face they coach us to rouse our courage, shame us to expose our lies, or quote

---

2   Spurgeon, *Autobiography*, Chapter 50, p. 234.

the Bible to stir our faith. They try to reason with us using 'logic' to demonstrate and prove the absurdity of our fears.

Choosing this tone of rebuke proves that they do not understand their fellow man or woman. Only in exasperated moments will some of them finally admit this. At the top of their lungs, or within their own whispered tears, they cry, "I just don't understand you!" "This just doesn't make any sense!"

Lack of control causes such persons to turn hastily to these tools of suspicion, judgment, condemnation, or misguided spiritual exhortation in order to fix the situation. But these tools simply do not work for this kind of painful thing. Instead, they will have to learn to use a different kind of tool. Otherwise, they will just keep kicking the broken-down stove, hoping to will its power to no avail. A painful foot and a dented friend are all the result that such tantrums will produce.

What then do we need to aid our understanding? Charles' story can help our own.

Depression Is A Kind Of Mental Arthritis
As Charles preached about depression, many troubled persons began to write to him. He felt like "a doctor who suddenly had a new practice handed over to him."[3] Out of this experience as caregiver as well as from his own experience with depression, he shared what he learned.

According to Charles, trite sayings and quick fixes will not work. Most sufferers cannot "be dismissed with just a word of hope and a dose of medicine, but require a long time in which to tell their griefs and to receive their

---

3   Charles Spurgeon, "A Stanza of Deliverance," *in the Metropolitan Tabernacle Pulpit*, Vol. 38 (Ages Digital Library, 1998), p. 65.

comfort." An "easy work and a hasty word" will not do. No matter how much sympathy we offer, it doesn't help. In short, depression reminds us that "there is a limit to human power ... God alone can take away the iron when it enters into the soul."[4]

We also have to recognize our own vulnerabilities as caregivers and sufferers. Speaking of a time in which he met with "several mournful cases of depression" in one day, he began to spiral down mentally and emotionally. "What must we do in such cases?" He asked, "Run away from these sorrowful ones? By no means!" But grace must secure our hope, otherwise we too "will soon feel that the sunlight has gone."[5] Both the sufferer and the one trying to help can be weighed down with the helpless feeling of it all and even suffer guilt and shame for it.

Perhaps, nothing in life reminds us that we are not God, and that this earth is not heaven, like an indescribable distress that sometimes defies cause and has no immediate cure, or no cure at all. There is likewise no harder moment, no more difficult chair on which to sit, than the one in which we await the doctor, when she, for all of her ordered tests upon our fatigued and needle-pricked flesh, must nonetheless admit to us: "we just don't know." How much more, then, when pain snipes at us from hidden positions within the bombed-out rubble of our minds?

With this kind of realism, Charles collaborates with "the wisest" helpers, who do not fail to acknowledge "the hard truth that serious depressions do not disappear

---

4   Spurgeon, "A Stanza of Deliverance," p. 65.

5   Charles Spurgeon, "Fever and Its Cure," *MTP*, Vol. 36 (Ages Digital Library, 1998), p. 796.

overnight."[6] Depression is best understood rather as "a kind of mental arthritis".[7] Unlike other sorrows this one infects us with malignant patience. Often we who suffer it have no ready or immediate rescue off of its stranded island. Rather, we must learn the skills of grace necessary for surviving there and adjusting our lives to what it means to thrive within its conditions.

But why won't the diagnoses solve it? It helps the sufferers to know what it is that haunts them. This kind of naming can relieve them. It also helps the caregiver and friend to grasp that something real and hard happens to their friend. But why so often doesn't the naming go further into fixing it? Perhaps it can help us to remember an analogy. A husband and wife can name their need for love, but we all know that the naming itself does not solve, but only labels, their needy experience. Naming depression is like this. It labels but does not solve. Why?

Unknown Causes and Simplistic Words

First of all, a cure doesn't come easily because, for all of our diagnoses, often the true cause remains hidden. "There is a kind of mental darkness," Charles observes, "in which you are disturbed, perplexed, worried, troubled – not, perhaps, about anything tangible."[8]

Just as King David cried out to himself, "Why are you cast down, O my soul? And why are you disquieted within me?," so we too argue with ourselves trying to find out

---

6   William Styron, *Darkness Visible: A Memoir of Madness* (New York: Vintage Books, 1992), p. 11.

7   David Karp, "An Unwelcome Career," in *Unholy Ghost: Writers on Depression*, ed., Nell Casey (New York: HarperCollins, 2001), p. 148.

8   Charles Spurgeon, "Night and Jesus Not There!" *MTP*, Vol. 51 (Ages Digital Library, 1998), p. 457.

the reason why we see and imagine foul tidings when none actually exist. "You can hardly tell why you are so depressed," he says, "if you could give a reason for your despondency, you might more easily get over it."[9]

Secondly, the inability to find adequate language doesn't help either. In his *Darkness Visible: A Memoir of Madness*, William Styron, observes that such an "ancient affliction" is often "indescribable".[10] The sufferer cannot find adequate language and congruently the would-be-helper simply has no ability "to imagine a form of torment so alien to everyday experience."[11] Explanations in this case are like holding a small lit-match within a system of night caverns beneath the ground; so small the light, so large the dark.

In sum, our words have limits. To diagnose cancer enables us to use the word "cancer" and to relate accordingly. But, naming the thing doesn't remove our having to endure it daily or our friends from having to relate with us as we do.

> Anybody who's ever *really* been sick knows that the tolerance level for illness is low. Once the get-well roses begin to wilt, everything changes. Compassion and caretaking turn into burdens and vulnerability becomes weakness. If the illness is something as nebulous as depression, folks begin to treat it like a character flaw: you are lazy, incapable, selfish, self absorbed.[12]

9   Charles Spurgeon, "Binding Up Broken Hearts," *MTP*, Vol. 54 (Ages Digital Library, 1998), p. 491.

10   William Styron, *Darkness Visible: A Memoir of Madness* (New York, New York: Vintage Books, 1992), pp. 16-17.

11   ibid.

12   Meri Nana-Ama Danquah, "Writing the Wrongs of Identity," in *Unholy Ghost: Writers on Depression,* ed., Nell Casey (New York: HarperCollins, 2001), p. 176.

Charles says it this way: "Your friends tell you that you are nervous, and there is no doubt that you are, but that does not alter the case."[13]

In short, try to remember this. Diagnostic words like "depression" are invitations, not destinations. Once you've spoken them, your travel with a person has begun, not ended.

There Are No One Size Fits All Diagnoses

But why? When we use words that describe depression as a destination rather than an invitation we become prone to "drape over diverse sufferers a label that hides more than it reveals."[14] We begin to treat sufferers in general rather than as they actually are individually.

Just like myriads of people named Bob or Julie differ immensely in personality even though they all share the same name, so each person who shares the diagnosis of "depression" differs in kind. Like a snowflake, though similar textures and patterns exist for identification, no two depressions are equally alike. "Each case is as different as each person's suffering,"[15] which means that "One person's panacea is another's trap."[16]

If sufferers from depression encounter us seeing them as a category, they disbelieve that we see them at all. Not at first, mind you. At first, the naming and the categories give romantic hope. They are often desperate for any kind of relief, even illusory ones. But soon enough, they

13   Charles Spurgeon, "Fainting," *MTP*, Vol. 49 (Ages Digital Library, 1998), p. 9.

14   Shenk, *Unholy Ghost*, p. 245.

15   Rose Styron, "Strands," in *Unholy Ghost: Writers on Depression*, ed., Nell Casey (New York: HarperCollins, 2001), p. 137.

16   Styron, *Darkness Visible*, p. 72.

discover that the naming does not heal. Something deeper has to occur. Veteran sufferers will no longer trust a mere category-dispenser as a caregiver.

According to Dr. Richard Winter, "Without realistic hope, all is lost." Realistic hope is "the door out of the blackness of depression and despair."[17] If our hope is trite, those who've suffered long enough to get let down by all the answers that people have offered them along the way, will see through to the emptiness of the hope we offer them.

What Do We Learn?

1. *For the sufferer, causes and cures may evade you for a while.* Charles says plainly: "You may be surrounded with all the comforts of life, and yet be in wretchedness more gloomy than death if the spirits be depressed. You may have no outward cause whatever for sorrow, and yet if the mind be dejected, the brightest sunshine will not relieve your gloom. At such a time, you may be vexed with cares, haunted with dread, and scared with things that distract you."[18]

2. *For the caregiver, our ability to help is real but also limited.* Sometimes, we try to address one concern only to discover that it has moved and another has taken its place. "You feel like Hercules cutting off the ever-growing heads of the Hydra. You give up your task in despair ... the more you try to comfort" the worse things get.[19]

---

17 Winter, *Roots of Sorrow*, p. 292.

18 Spurgeon, "The Frail Leaf."

19 Charles Spurgeon, "The Comforter," Sermon 5 *NPSP, The Spurgeon Archive* (http://www.spurgeon.org/sermons/0005.htm), accessed 2/28, 14.

Consequently, we must pause here first and humbly admit our needy position. We are not omniscient. We cannot know everything. As the apostle Paul reminds us, we are like those who look upon God, each other, and the world, as through a dim mirror. We always see but only partially and vaguely (1 Cor. 13:12).

On this point, Charles reminds us to make it our aim always to give thanks to God for what we do see clearly, no matter how small, but thereby to "check our conceit." For "we know only in part," he says. "Beloved, the objects we look at are distant, and we are near-sighted.[20]"

A realistic hope teaches us to confess at the outset, then, that our limited ability to see includes our attempts to explain depression. There is no room for pride here. Grace from a story larger than this particular moment of gloom must have its way.

The Cane of His Grace
If a lame man is given a cane, he need not know who gave it to him, nor why his leg needs help, before he can make use of the cane's strength and take a walk in garden bloom.

Many fellow sufferers have made a good life without ever knowing exactly why the darkness haunted them so. When we do discover reasons why, we give thanks. But when reasons remain hidden, we learn to give thanks too, and limp, leaning upon the cane. Either way, grace beyond our sight sees us clear. It can bear well the weight that we cannot.

How then can we talk about a Cane of God's Grace in the midst of our excruciating inability to find cures, causes

---

20   Charles Spurgeon, "Now and Then," *MTP*, Sermon Number 1002 (http://www.spurgeon.org/sermons/1002.htm), accessed December 4, 2012.

or even comfort? Doesn't this kind of god-talk only further the trite and damaging ideas of an unrealistic hope?

6

A Language for our Sorrows

"He who now feebly expounds these words knows within himself more than he would care or dare to tell of the abysses of inward anguish .... Terrors are turned upon me, they pursue my soul as the wind."[1]

Jane Kenyon's remarkable poem, "Having it out with Melancholy," poses two "God" problems associated with depression and our attempts at care. First, depression ruins our "manners toward God" because it teaches us "to exist without gratitude," and tempts us to answer the purpose of our existence as "simply to wait for death," since "the pleasures of earth are overrated."[2] Second, depression

---

1   Charles Spurgeon, "Psalm 88," *The Treasury of David* (http://www.spurgeon. org/treasury/ps088.htm), accessed 3/17/14.

2   Jane Kenyon, "Having it Out with Melancholy" in *Jane Kenyon: Collected Poems* (Saint Paul, Minnesota: Grey Wolf Press, 2005), p. 231.

tempts our friends to offer the following advice: "You wouldn't be so depressed if you really believed in God."[3]

To learn from Kenyon's painful truths, we first need a gracious re-acquaintance with the manners of God toward the depressed. So, in this chapter we will explore the gracious language that God gives to the suffering. Then, in the next chapter, we will explore the kind of help in God's name that does more harm than good.

Let's start then with the gracious language that God gives to the sufferer of sorrows. In this we see His kind manners toward us even when our manners toward Him seemed shipwrecked and lost at sea.

The Bible Uses Metaphors to Aid the Sorrowing

Sufferers of depression lean on metaphors. Andrew Solomon explains why. Since "depression is a condition that is almost unimaginable to anyone who has not known it," its diagnosis "depends on metaphors".[4]

Solomon then highlights the commonly used metaphors for depression of going over the edge of a cliff or falling into an abyss. William Styron likewise leaned upon the images of drowning and suffocation to attempt description of his affliction. Which metaphor would you use?

Charles acts no differently. According to him, our depressions of various kinds make us like those who "traverse" the "howling desert".[5] We endure "winters".[6] We

---

3   Kenyon, "Having it Out with Melancholy", p. 232.

4   Andrew Solomon, *The Noonday Demon: An Atlas of Depression* (New York: Scribner, 2003), 499 of 13854.

5   Charles Spurgeon, "A Call to the Depressed," *MTP*, Vol. 60 (Ages Digital Library), p. 542.

6   Charles Spurgeon, "Sweet Stimulants for the Fainting Soul," *MTP*, Vol. 48 (Ages Digital Library), p. 578.

are "bruised as a cluster, trodden in the wine-press" and we enter the "foggy day", amid storms like those "caught in a hurricane".[7] "The waters roll continually wave upon wave" over the tops of us.[8] We are like those "haunted with dread",[9] in the "dark dungeon"[10] or "sitting in a chimney-corner under an accumulation ... of pains, and weaknesses, and sorrows."[11] We "sit in darkness, like one who is chilled and benumbed, and over whom death is slowly creeping."[12] We are as "panting warriors" and "poor fainting soldiers"[13] crying out for relief from this "long fight of affliction".[14]

Historian Stanley W. Jackson wrote about this necessary use of metaphor in his *Melancholia & Depression: From Hippocratic Times to Modern Times*. Jackson found "no literal statement", no one-word diagnosis, that was able to describe adequately the diversity of our sadnesses along with their varying fits of gloom and mood. What he found instead were two recurring word-pictures: "being in a state of darkness and being weighed down."[15]

---

7   Charles Spurgeon, "All Day Long," *MTP*, Vol. 36 (Ages Digital Library), p. 433.

8   Charles Spurgeon, *Faith's Checkbook* (Ages Digital Library), p. 4.

9   Charles Spurgeon, "The Frail Leaf," *MTP*, Vol. 57 (Ages Digital Library), p. 590.

10 Charles Spurgeon, "The Shank Bone Sermon; Or, True Believers and Their Helpers," *MTP, Vol.* 36 (Ages Digital Library), p. 252.

11 Charles Spurgeon, "Faintness and Refreshing," *MTP*, Vol. 54 (Ages Digital Library), p. 592.

12 Charles Spurgeon, "A Discourse to the Despairing," *MTP*, Vol. 40 (Ages Digital Library), p. 616.

13 Charles Spurgeon, "The Fainting Warrior," *PSP*, Vol. 5 (Ages Digital Library), pp. 145-6.

14 Charles Spurgeon, "Faint, But Not Fainthearted," *MTP*, Vol. 40 (Ages Digital Library), p. 23.

15 Quoted in Joshua Shenk, "A Melancholy of My Own," in *Unholy Ghost: Writers on Depression*, ed., Nell Casey (New York: HarperCollins, 2002), p. 249.

Charles found such metaphors and similes preceding him in the Bible itself. In its pages the faithful describe their inward condition in terms of pits and miry bogs, deep shadows and grave-lands, floodwaters that swallow us whole. The Psalmist leans upon such language.

> For my soul is full of troubles ...
>   I am a man who has no strength,
> like one set loose among the dead,
>   like the slain that lie in the grave,
> like those whom you remember no more,
>   for they are cut off from your hand.
> You have put me in the depths of the pit,
>   in the regions dark and deep ...
> you overwhelm me with all your waves. (Ps. 88:3-7)

Metaphor becomes our teacher of prayer. Our prayers from the depth of our hearts begin to sound like this:

> Let not the flood sweep over me,
>   or the deep swallow me up,
>   or the pit close its mouth over me (Ps. 69:15).

Even Charles' sermon titles began to utilize the metaphors that Scripture offers for the sorrowing; titles such as "the frail leaf" (Job. 13:25)[16], the "wounded spirit" (Prov. 18:14, KJV), the "fainting soul" (Ps. 42:6)[17], and "the bruised reed" (Isa. 42:1-3). Jesus is "the man of sorrows" (Isa. 53:3). He does not quit us amid the agony of a fleshly thorn (2 Cor. 12:7).

Metaphor Can Handle the Mystery

What implication does God's manner of using metaphor

---

16   Spurgeon's version of these portions of Scripture. See copyright page.
17   Ibid.

have for us? You and I need a language of sorrows and God teaches it to us. But why do we need such an apprenticeship?

The poet Wendell Berry once described his intention to write his farming poems with language suitable to the place. His aim was that if one were to read his poems and then visit the place from which the poems were formed, the language of the poem would prove native rather than foreign to the place itself.[18]

Likewise, when we look to the language of God given in the Bible, we find within it a language that the miserable would recognize as native and not foreign to the geography of their inward anguish. We begin gradually to speak and to refrain from speaking as those who know this terrain of anguish first hand. When such speaking takes place, realistic hope has a chance.

Metaphor grows native to the terrain of depression because:

(1) Metaphor leaves room. It does not propose to cover every angle, understand every possibility or to explain every detail. It does not require only one possible explanation. Language that proposes to do this with depression exposes its ignorance of the situation at hand.

(2) Metaphor allows for nuance and difference. Since each person's experience with depression differs, metaphor allows for diverse expression. Formulaic prose or platitudes immediately reveal their lack of realism regarding how depression damages someone.

(3) Metaphor requires further thought and exploration. It is a word of invitation more than destination which, we

---

18   Wendell Berry, "Notes from an Absence and Return," in *A Continuous Harmony* (Washington, D.C.: Shoemaker & Hoard, 1972),pp. 35-36.

observed earlier, is crucial for gathering up the debris of depression.

Without metaphor, depression often exposes the inexperience of our vocabulary. It lays bare our bias toward the happy, prosaic or clinical words assumed by our impatience or our theological training or our medical preferences. It uncovers the sobering prejudice against lament so popular in our god-talk and our failed attempts to care well.

Realistic hope, in contrast, counts on the use of metaphor. With it, we create a poetry of sorrows, a dictionary of sadnesses. Realistic hope teaches us the capacity to enter the "crowding gloom," the "gathering murk," "the poisonous mood," "the howling tempest in the brain," "the interior doom," that attends many of our neighbors.[19] Our language for darkness grows helpful. Our capacity to love a neighbor deepens.

Without this, we offer mere band-aids to the broken-boned, topical lotion for the internal bleeder. We describe the choking gray breath of a wheezing anxiety with pastels. And then when thorns and thistles take over, all of our balloon words pop.

At this point, Kathleen Norris startles us by pointing out a penetrating irony. She laments that if we want to find words that create suitable paths on which to walk, "You're better off with poets than with Christians." She says, "It's ironic, because the scriptures of the Christian canon are full of strange metaphors that create their own reality."[20]

Sometimes those of us who suffer depression feel the sting of this irony – the inability to find empathy and

---

19   William Styron, *Darkness Visible: A Memoir of Madness* (New York: Vintage Books, 1992), pp. 12, 14, 24, 38, 45.

20   Kathleen Norris, *The Cloister Walk* (New York: Penguin, 1996), pp. 154-5.

comfort from the very people who read the Bible every day but do not recognize the gift of metaphor for the sorrowing within its pages. How can we lessen the sting of an unrealistic hope?

1. As a sufferer, *search for metaphors to describe your experience.* Receive the metaphors that fellow sufferers have spoken as the whispered gifts of good friends. Receive the gracious manner of God in filling the scriptures with a poetry for the sorrowing as His ability to sit knowledgeably and empathetically in the ashes with you.

2. As a caregiver, *learn patience and appreciation for metaphor.* You have admitted that no easy answer or fix is available and that your wordy prose of explanation or exhortation cannot remedy the situation. But this does not mean that words are of no use to you. Words of a certain kind offer you great use. Metaphor invites us to say, "What does that mean?" To ask such a question and then to listen and learn is to use words as invitations and bridges toward empathy and shared understanding.

Poetry from God for our Sorrows

With this history of metaphor and story recorded in the scriptures, the soul-dashed, the broken-brained and the devil-spooked are given a larger story and a suitable language.

At this point we return to the question that we've been asking. How can we locate a larger story about God for our sorrows without being cruel or trite about it? For Charles, it was partly because the language of God reveals a Being who truly understands our plight.

If Charles is right, and God is truly gracious to give language for our sorrows, then a realistic hope begins to sweep faintly but truly into view like waves at tide rolling beneath our night skies. Such hope pulses and fades, like the lighthouse lamp slowly circling out of view. Into sight it returns, again then again, relentlessly pushing its way through the fog and absence toward us. The night waters begin to shimmer with promise.

> There will be no gloom for her who was in anguish ....
> The people who walked in darkness
>   have seen a great light;
> those who dwelt in a land of deep darkness,
>   on them has light shone. (Isa. 9:1ff)

A larger story about God exists that possesses within it a language of sorrows so that the gloomy, the anguished, the dark-pathed, and the inhabitants of deep night are given voice. Such a god-story is neither cruel nor trite. Such a story begins to reveal the sympathy of God.

Divine sympathy is your teacher, dear caregiver; your ally and friend, dear sufferer. Let His sorrow's language help you.

7

The Help that Harms

"Ah!" says one, "I used to laugh at Mrs. So-and-so for being nervous; now that I feel the torture myself, I am sorry that I was ever hard on her." "Ah!" says another, "I used to think of such-and-such a person that he must be a fool to be always in so gloomy a state of mind; but now I cannot help sinking into the same desponding frames, and oh! I would to God that I had been more kind to him!" Yes, we should feel more for the prisoner if we knew more about the prison.[1]

We are asking a question about God at the moment. How can we place our sorrows into a larger story about God, when so often people use such god-talk to cruelly or tritely treat us? We've answered first by looking at the language of sorrows given through metaphor, which saturates scripture's pages. Now we turn our attention to another part of this larger story about God. We've hinted at this all

---

1   Charles Spurgeon, "A Troubled Prayer," *MTP*, Sermon 741, *Christian Classics Ethereal Library* (http://www.ccel.org/ccel/spurgeon/sermons13.xiv.html), accessed 12/13/13.

along, but now let's look plainly at this truth. Not only has God given us a gracious language suitable for our sorrows, but as Charles saw it, God also advocates for the sorrowing by exposing the kind of help that harms us.

Why We Are Harsh With Sufferers

According to Charles, it is a fact that "strong minded people are very apt to be hard upon nervous folk," and "to speak harshly to people who are very depressed in spirit," saying, 'really, you ought to rouse yourself out of that state.'"[2]

The result is that a strong person says to a poor suffering one, "Stuff and nonsense! Try to exert yourself!" But when he does this, he says "one of the most cruel things that can be said to the sufferer." By trying to help he "only inflicts additional pain."[3]

What accounts for our tendency of impatient care toward depression?

1. *We judge others according to our circumstances rather than theirs.* "There are a great many of you who appear to have a large stock of faith, but it is only because you are in very good health and your business is prospering. If you happened to get a disordered liver, or your business should fail, I should not be surprised if nine parts out of ten of your wonderful faith should evaporate."[4] Jesus teaches us about those who lay up heavy burdens on others but do not lift a finger to help (Matt. 23:4).

---

2   Charles Spurgeon, "The Saddest Cry from the Cross," *MTP*, Vol. 48 (Ages Digital Library, 1998), p. 663.

3   Charles Spurgeon, "Binding Up Broken Hearts," *MTP*, Vol. 491, (http://www.ccel.org/ccel/spurgeon/sermons54.xxxii.html), accessed 8/15/14.

4   Charles Spurgeon, "Night and Jesus Not There," in *MTP*, Vol. 51 (Ages Digital Library, 1998), p. 457.

2. *We still think that trite sayings or a raised voice can heal deep wounds.* A person "may have a great spiritual sorrow, and someone who does not at all understand his grief, may proffer to him a consolation which is far too slight." Like a physician who offers a common ointment for a deep wound, we "say to a person in deep distress things which have really aggravated him and his malady too."[5] In this regard, Charles teaches us the Scriptures, "Whoever sings songs to a heavy heart is like one who takes off a garment on a cold day, and like vinegar on soda" (Prov. 25:20).

3. *We try to control what should be rather than surrender to what is.* We must not "judge harshly, as if things were as we would theoretically arrange them, but we must deal with things as they are, and it cannot be questioned that some of the best believers are at times sorely put to it," even "to know whether they are believers at all."[6] The Scriptures teach us about Job's friends who struggled at this very point.

4. *We resist humility regarding our own lack of experience.* "There are some people who cannot comfort others, even though they try to do so, because they never had any troubles themselves. It is a difficult thing for a man who has had a life of uninterrupted prosperity to sympathize with another whose path has been exceedingly rough."[7] The Apostle Paul teaches us to comfort others out of

5   Charles Spurgeon, "Refusing to Be Comforted," *MTP*, Vol. 44 (Ages Digital Library, 1998), p. 417.

6   Charles Spurgeon, "Helps to Full Assurance," *MTP*, Vol. 30 (Ages Digital Library, 1998), p. 516.

7   Charles Spurgeon, "Binding Up Broken Hearts," *MTP*, Vol. 54 (Ages Digital Library, 1998), p. 491.

the comfort that we ourselves have needed and received (2 Cor. 1:4).

According to the Bible, when we encounter someone who weeps, we too are meant to weep (Rom. 12:15). When someone encounters adversity they are meant to reflect and meditate, and we with them (Eccles. 7:14). Without this together-sympathy our attempts to help others can lose the sound of reality. The loss of this sound of reality forges the larger reason for our harshness.

The Sound of Reality

When we suffer depression, we wish that our preachers, Christian coffee shop talkers and answer-givers knew more about the prison in which we suffer before they proposed to speak about it.

One of Spurgeon's contemporaries said it this way. A god-talker and a religious answer-giver must "have a *sound of reality* in the ears of victims such as these." The salvation and rescue which such preachers and counselors propose to those who suffer "must come in as strong a form as the complaint" itself, if the message is to "take effect."[8]

Our salvation messages will prove inadequate if they do not meaningfully account for the large portions of reality that cause screaming in the world; particularly with depression. It has long been recognized that a spirituality focused only on sunshine, positive thinking, immediacy and quick-fix Bible quoting "breaks down impotently as soon as melancholy comes."[9] When we attempt to help sufferers of depression

---

8   William James, *The Varieties of Religious Experience* (New York: Barnes & Noble Classics, 2004), pp. 147, 148. (italics mine).

9   ibid.

without this kind of reality in our words, they will not be able to hear us because they will think that we have not yet heard them. The gospel we offer them will seem unable to handle the depth of what they actually experience in real life.

The Rupture of Meaning

What sufferers experience is "a meaning rupture" within their lives. The larger story seems fractured or unknowable. Meaning-ruptures happen to most of us. "On one side," Jennifer Michael Hecht says, "there is a world in our heads ... a world of reason and plans, love, and purpose. On the other side there is the world beyond our human life—an equally real world in which there is no sign of caring or value, planning or judgment, love or joy."[10]

But now imagine how this rupture of meaning feels to sufferers of depression, when "the world in our heads" is filled not with "reason, plans, love and purpose" but with the loss of reasons, plans, love and purpose. In this state, both the world out there and the one within conspire miserably to deny hope. Both the floor and ceiling vanish. We free-fall with no place to land. When realistic hope quits, so do we. Charles nearly did, and this more than once.

Therefore, when true meaning to our experience ruptures, we must hold on to what William James called "the remoter schemes and hopes of life."[11] By "remoter schemes," James referred to what we might call "a larger story" in which our current melancholy signifies only a scene or a chapter.

When the remoter scheme, or the meta-narrative, goes dark, and we have no larger story in which to place our

---

10 Jennifer Michael Hecht, *Doubt: A History* (New York: HarperCollins, 2004), p. xii.

11 James, *The Varieties of Religious Experience*, p. 130.

present gloom, "the proximity of despair"[12] intensifies, and so therefore must the realism of our hope.

In short, the hope that we offer must match the depths of the wound and the misery of the pain. What difference would this make in our self-care and in our caregiving?

We Change the Way We Care

First, we are going to slow down and take a longer view. We are going to be at this for a while. The solution isn't just a matter of getting the words right.

Second, matching the depths changes the way we speak in public. People who suffer depression and other mental challenges are always near us. As a public speaker, Charles worked hard to use language that could match the intensity of despair. In Psalm 88 for example he highlighted verse 6 (KJV), which says: "Thou hast laid me in the lowest pit, in darkness, in the deeps."[13] He then lingered with these Scripture words. "What a collection of forcible metaphors," he observed. "None of the similes are strained." Then he told us why.

> The mind can descend far lower than the body, for in it there are bottomless pits. The flesh can bear only a certain number of wounds and no more, but the soul can bleed in ten thousand ways, and die over and over again each hour.[14]

Third, his personal ministry resembled his ministry in the pulpit. Sufferers of mind became a people to whom Charles regularly paid attention, even though he was a pastor with national and worldwide prominence. "In talking with those who are in a wretched condition, I find

---

12   Berry, *Life is a Miracle*, p. 7.

13   Charles Spurgeon, "Psalm 88," in *The Treasury of David, The Spurgeon Archive* (http://www.spurgeon.org/treasury/ps088.htm), accessed 12/13/13.

14   ibid.

myself at home," he said. "He who has been in the dark dungeon knows the way to the bread and the water."[15]

Such personal and pulpit ministry created a challenge at times. Even when he tried to find time for personal retreat and vacation, "it seemed as if all who were suffering from depression of spirit, whether living in Mentone, Nice, Cannes, Bordighera, or San Remo, found him out, and sought the relief which his sympathetic heart was ever ready to bestow."[16]

The result resembles what any caregiver will feel. "It is not easy to lift others up without finding yourself exhausted."[17] Grace upon grace forges our mantra and our need. Grace that never tires forges our hope.

The Larger Story of God

Back when the prankster yelled "fire!" and people died while Spurgeon preached, the young husband and father of twin one-month-olds was put on what we would call today a "suicide watch." "I was so unmanned by it," he recalls. "Someone watched me, for they did not know what might happen to me."[18] "I had almost lost my reason for some three weeks."[19]

---

15 Charles Spurgeon, "The Shank-Bone Sermon; Or , True Believers and their Helpers ," *MTP*, Vol. 36 (Ages Digital Library, 1998), p. 252.

16 Charles Spurgeon, *Autobiography Vol. 4* (http://www.grace-ebooks.com/library/Charles%20Spurgeon/CHS_Autobiography/CHS_Autobiography%20Vol%204.PDF), p. 233 accessed 3/18/14.

17 Charles Spurgeon, "Fever and its Cure," *MTP*, Vol. 36 (http://www.ccel.org/ccel/spurgeon/sermons36.lii.html), accessed 3/18/14.

18 Charles Spurgeon, "Joy in Place of Sorrow," *MTP*, Vol. 43 (Ages Digital Library, 1998), p. 446.

19 Charles Spurgeon, "Belief in the Resurrection," *MTP*, Vol. 61 (Ages Digital Library, 1998), p. 148.

But looking back, Charles connects these helpless scenes of his loss of reason within this larger story about God, both in the world and in his life. Charles says to his congregation:

> Do you recollect how you cried for your minister, that he might be restored to a reason that was then tottering? Do you remember how God has been with us? We have had special work, special trial, special deliverance.[20]

"Our perspective on what is happening is vital to our sense of hope. So much depression arises because of a loss of perspective."[21] When we no longer expect that a realistic way of help can come, we lose hope.

So, we return to the question we've been asking. How can we entrust our sorrows to the larger story of God?

We are beginning to make an attempt at answering this important question now. God has the sound of reality about Him when He relates to us in our sorrows and sufferings. He knows firsthand the proximity of our despair. He gives us language and care proportionate to our pains.

Now, we want to take a moment and see why Jesus means so much to this larger story in general and for us who suffer from depression in particular.

---

20 Charles Spurgeon, *Autobiography*, Chapter 50 (Ages Digital Library, 1998), p. 235.

21 Richard Winter, *The Roots of Sorrow: Reflections on Depression and Hope* (Crossway Books, 1986), p. 292.

8

Jesus and Depression

*"It is an unspeakable consolation that our Lord
Jesus knows this experience."*[1]

In *The Noonday Demon: An Atlas of Depression*, Andrew Solomon, who does not profess to follow Jesus, nonetheless observes that "even those people whose faith promises them that this will all be different in the next world cannot help experiencing anguish in this one; Christ himself was the man of sorrows."[2]

This phrase "man of sorrows" comes from Isaiah 53:3. The Old Testament prophet describes the promised One from God. Charles testified regularly to the blessed

---

1   Winter, *The Roots of Sorrow: Reflections on Depression and Hope*, p. 292.

2   Solomon, *The Noonday Demon: An Atlas of Depression*, p. 15.

strength that relationship with Jesus as the man of sorrows afforded him.

> Personally, I also bear witness that it has been to me, in seasons of great pain, superlatively comfortable to know that in every pang which racks his people the Lord Jesus has a fellow-feeling. We are not alone, for one like unto the Son of man walks the furnace with us.[3]

Jesus Suffered Depression Too

The "fellow-feeling" that sufferers find in the larger story of Jesus includes those of us who suffer depression. Christians are used to being students of the Cross. But Charles invites sufferers to find our Savior's help in the garden of Gethsemane.

This "garden of sorrow"[4] becomes for Charles a picture of the "mental depression" of Jesus.[5] "Bodily pain should help us to understand the cross," Charles says, but "mental depression should make us apt scholars at Gethsemane."[6] "The sympathy of Jesus is the next most precious thing to his sacrifice."[7] Caregivers do well here to take notice.

So, when the New Testament book of Hebrews says that Jesus is "one who in every respect has been tempted as we are" and "because he himself has suffered when tempted, he is able to help those who are being tempted (Heb. 4:15; 2:18),

---

3   Charles Spurgeon, "The Man of Sorrows," *MTP*, Vol. 19 (Ages Digital Library, 1998), p. 153.

4   Charles Spurgeon, "The Weakened Christ Strengthened," *MTP* , Vol. 48 (Ages Digital Library, 1998), p. 149.

5   Charles Spurgeon, "Gethsemane," *MTP*, Vol. 9 (Ages Digital Library, 1998), 103. See also, "The Overflowing Cup," in Vol. 15, p. 388.

6   Charles Spurgeon, "The Overflowing Cup," *MTP*, Vol. 15 (Ages Digital Library, 1998), p. 388.

7   Spurgeon, "The Man of Sorrows," p. 154.

Charles readily applies this sympathy of Jesus to include not only our physical weakness but also our "mental depression".[8]

The result? Sufferers of depression can find a place to rest within the storyline of Jesus. "How completely it takes the bitterness out of grief," Charles explains, "to know that it once was suffered by him."[9]

Because of this, when we grow numb toward god-talkers whose hope isn't realistic or who know nothing of what we experience, we needn't bypass Jesus. On the contrary, when we search for someone, anyone, to know what it means to walk in our shoes, Jesus emerges as the preeminent and truest companion for our afflictions. Realistic hope is a Jesus-saturated thing. Those who suffer depression have an ally, a hero, a companion-redeemer, advocating for the mentally harassed.

Finding Comfort in Jesus

At this point, it might surprise us that heaven is not always the best consolation for those in depression. In fact, when we are conscious only of our misery, it sometimes offers little consolation to attempt comfort by constantly referring to the great by and by. In these times, "The afflicted do not so much look for comfort to Christ as he will come a second time ... as to Christ as he came the first time, a weary man and full of woes."[10] Why? Because, we ourselves are weary and full of woe with no finishing line in sight.

By saying this, Charles does not dismiss the future advocacy of Jesus. Certainly a vision of Jesus with us and for us in heaven can sometimes bring relief to our misery. In Him, we see that our present sufferings are light and momentary. He will outlast our suffering and in Him so will we!

8   Spurgeon, "The Weakened Christ Strengthened," p. 143.

9   Spurgeon, "The Man of Sorrows," p. 154.

10   Spurgeon, "The Man of Sorrows," p. 149.

Likewise, Charles doesn't dismiss the present advocacy of Jesus either. "Oh, how it would cheer you up at any time when you were depressed, only to see him standing and pleading for you!" he says.[11] The presence of Jesus defending us, holding us secure, never abandoning us, provides immense comfort. His presence is good news!

But Charles highlights a vital point that sometimes "even the glories of Christ afford no such consolation to afflicted spirits." Instead, what we need to know for ourselves in our hearts is that Jesus is "The Chief Mourner who above all others could say, 'I am the man that hath seen affliction.'"[12] To feel in our being that the God to whom we cry has Himself suffered as we do enables us to feel that we are not alone and that God is not cruel.

Therefore, in Jesus, it is neither trite nor cruel to speak of God's larger story for the sake of our own, because this God is like a near king in battle. He is not like those royal but distant ones who sit in the back eating in luxury while their soldiers suffer a cause for which they themselves will not personally lift a finger. In such cases, like those soldiers we would grow weary and resigned.

But in Jesus we have no distant God story. On the contrary, this King leads from the front. He hungers when His people do. He thirsts when they thirst. He puts aside the cup of water offered to Him, passing it to a fellow soldier who looks more faint than Himself. Therefore, we who see Him fight and suffer among us begin to believe that we too can endure because He does. We cry out, "This day, assuredly, we can bear poverty, slander, contempt or bodily pain, or death itself;

---

11   Charles Spurgeon, "Honey in the Mouth," Sermon 2213 *MTP, The Spurgeon Archive* (http://www.spurgeon.org/sermons/2213.htm), accessed 2/26/14.

12   ibid., p. 150.

because Jesus Christ our Lord has borne it." Why? Because "if there be consolation anywhere, surely it is to be found in the delightful presence of the Crucified."[13] "Ordinary mourners ... sip at sorrow's bowl, but he drains it dry."[14]

We rightly wonder why God allows depression and other suffering. But let us also wonder why He chooses to suffer it with us and for us. The "man of sorrows" reveals a larger story of God, which possesses the capacity for realistic hope amid our proximity of despair. But what are some of the ways in which this larger story shapes our attentiveness to depression?

Dealing with our Highs and Lows

One Sunday morning, Charles shared openly in his sermon. "This week has been in some respects the crowning week of my life," he said, "but it closed with a horror of great darkness of which I will say no more than this."[15] Charles then speaks of his propensity for highs and lows. "I suppose that some brethren neither have much elevation or depression. I could almost wish to share their peaceful life." He continues: "For I am much tossed up and down, and although my joy is greater than the most of men, my depression of spirit is such as few can have an idea of."[16]

Charles shared this personal testimony as an illustration of the reference he made to the Old Testament prophet, Elijah. Following an unprecedented success in Elijah's life, terrible depression followed. So much so that Elijah asked to die. "High exaltations involve deep depressions," Charles quips. Then he turns to apply this truth directly

---

13   ibid.

14   ibid., p. 155.

15   Charles Spurgeon, "Israel's God and God's Israel," *MTP*, Vol. 14 (Ages Digital Library, 1998), p. 238.

16   Charles Spurgeon, "Israel's God and God's Israel," *MTP*, Vol. 14, p. 238.

to those who likewise know what it means "to fall into the depths of depression." He applies the care of the near God to our daily abyss.

- *No matter how deep you fall, grace goes deeper still.* "What was under Elijah when he fell down in that fainting fit under the juniper tree? Why, underneath were the everlasting arms." No matter how far you fall in your depression, "the eternal arms shall be lower than you are."[17]

- *Grace goes deeper no matter what the cause.* "Brethren, there are many such occasions in which the spirit sinks sometimes through a sense of sin, through disappointments, through desertions of friends, through beholding the decay of the Lord's work, through a lack of success in our ministry, or a thousand other mischiefs which may all cast us low."[18] Jesus is able to sympathize and recover us no matter what we face.

In another sermon, Charles similarly revealed his condition. "I am quite out of order for addressing you tonight. I feel extremely unwell, excessively heavy and exceedingly depressed."[19] But what aided him that night was "the pleasure of trying to say a few words" about the gospel to those who gathered. The pleasure of telling the larger story of Jesus' suffering and sympathy can mysteriously strengthen us in our depression.

We Learn to Tell Our Stories
Why did Charles talk about his depression so openly? He braved those who would stigmatize, shame or discriminate

17 Charles Spurgeon, "Israel's God and God's Israel," *MTP*, Vol. 14, p. 238.
18 ibid.
19 Charles Spurgeon, *Sword and Trowel 1869* (Ages Digital Library, 1998), p. 9.

him. How? Because just as the story of Jesus tells us of the God who has been there in order to give us realistic hope, we who've been there with Him learn to tell our stories too. In the midst of the pit we doubt that our story could matter to anyone, much less to God or to ourselves. But in truth, those who've traversed the howling desert have things to say that no one else really can.

1. *We tell our stories, not for sympathy, or to steal another's story for our own attention, but to sympathize.* "Sharp bodily pain succeeded mental depression and this was accompanied both by bereavement and affliction in the person of one dear as life. The waters rolled in continually, wave upon wave. I do not mention this to exact sympathy, but simply to let the reader see that I am no dry-land sailor.... I know the roll of the billows and the rush of the winds."[20]

2. *We tell our stories not because we wanted this experience but because we've had this experience.* "'Well,' says one, 'I do not want to feel that sort of treatment.' No, but suppose you had felt it, the next time you meet with a brother who was locked up in the castle of Giant Despair, you would know how to sympathize with him."[21]

3. *We tell our stories so that sufferers know that Jesus feels, not for their strengths but for their infirmities.* "Our pain, our depression, our trembling, our sensitiveness; he is touched with these, though he falls not into the sin which too often comes of them. Hold fast this truth, for it may greatly tend to your consolation on another day. Jesus is touched, not with a feeling of

20   Charles Spurgeon, *Faith's Checkbook* (Ages Digital Library, 1998), p. 4.

21   Charles Spurgeon, "A Stanza of Deliverance," *MTP*, vol. 38 (Ages Digital Library, 1998), p. 72.

your strength, but of your infirmity ... as the mother feels with the weakness of her babe, so does Jesus feel with the poorest, saddest, and weakest" of His own.[22]

4. *We tell our stories to serve realistic hope.* "If you have passed through depression of mind, and the Lord has appeared to your comfort, lay yourself out to help others who are where you used to be."[23]

Returning to Kenyon's Poem

We started with Kenyon's poem awhile back. She talked about how depression ruins our manners with God and how god-talkers ruin their manners toward us. We've marveled at why Charles could suffer depression as he did and yet look to God as kind and present toward him.

Perhaps it is surprising to some of us. We think of the Bible as a violent book, of God as angry, and god-talkers as sloganeers. But Charles saw in the Bible a language for the sorrowing, an advocacy to disrupt helpers who harm, and a man of sorrows sent from God out of love for the wailing world so that those who sat in darkness could finally feel the home they were made for and enjoy the sun again. This remoter scheme or larger story became the means by which Charles daily reckoned with the proximity of his despair. God had offered a reason for hope that matched the intensity of our reasons for despondency.

How then does this God-narrative in Jesus inform the way we try to cope every day with our depression? After all, no quick fixes and trite sayings work, not even the religious kind. So, what difference in our daily life does this narrative offer to us?

---

22 Charles Spurgeon, "The Tenderness of Jesus," *MTP*, Vol. 36 (Ages Digital Library, 1998), p. 402.

23 Spurgeon, "The Shank-Bone Sermon," p. 252.

Part Three:

Learning Helps to Daily Cope with Depression

Part Three

9

Promises and Prayers

"An ointment for every wound, a cordial for every faintness, a remedy for every disease. Blessed is he who is well skilled in heavenly pharmacy and knows how to lay hold on the healing virtues of the promises of God!"[1]

Promises can rouse our cynicism. We once hoped in them, but now they resemble the throwaway pennies, scrap papers or leftover bolts shoved away in the junk drawer. The Psalmist gives us language in Psalm 77:8: "Has his steadfast love forever ceased? Are his promises at an end for all time?"

And yet, our need to reorient our lives around the risk of promises remains necessary, even if our relationship with

---

1   Charles Spurgeon, "Obtaining Promises," (http://www.ccel.org/ccel/spurgeon/sermons08.ix.html), accessed 3/26/14.

promises sometimes reveals only our painful questions about them. Why? Because promises of a certain kind are like voices of realistic hope that intrude into our dungeon thoughts. They are "precious and very great," given as gifts to us from God (2 Pet. 1:4). Our souls need them.

In the next chapter we will look at the natural helps available to us. Medicines, good humor, rest, communion with nature, warm baths, nutrition, and scheduling our days according to our limits, along with therapy and pastoral counsel, are made useful in the hands of the man of sorrows.

But first let's learn tenderly in Him to recognize God's promises as a sort of lighthouse reaching out into our night seas.

Writing Messages to Ourselves

It sounds strange but we will want to learn how to talk to ourselves about God's promises. One way to do this is to write notes to ourselves or for others to do so for us.

For example, sometimes a date on a calendar evokes painful memory or frightful imagination. We look ahead at the calendar and perhaps imagine all manner of doom. Charles encourages us to write promises in the margins of our calendars, such as Psalm 91:4: "He will cover you with his pinions, and under his wings you will find refuge."[2] Then, on the basis of that promise, Charles declares: "Let the unknown tomorrow bring with it what it may, it cannot bring us anything but what God shall bear us through."[3]

---

2   A *King James Version* slightly altered as quoted by Spurgeon. See copyright page.

3   Charles Spurgeon, "Safe Shelter," *MTP*, Vol. 15 (Ages Digital Library, 1998), p. 787.

Charles also posted notes of God's promises in his home. During a season of cruel criticisms and public slanders, his wife Susannah even framed Matthew 5:11-12 and hung this promise of Jesus in their bedroom for her husband to see every morning. "Blessed are ye, when men shall revile you, and persecute you, and shall say all manner of evil against you falsely, for my sake. Rejoice, and be exceedingly glad: for great is your reward in heaven: for so persecuted they the prophets which were before you" (KJV).

Charles urged others to live by God's promises too. He encouraged them to purchase a copy of Clarke's *Precious Promises*.[4] Charles kept his own personal copy of this book in his pocket so that he could appeal to it when pain of body or mind or anxiety began to do its foul disabling.[5] This little book of promises is arranged by headings that indicate various life circumstances and conditions. Under the heading "Support in Trouble" it lists Scriptures such as these:

- "Though I walk in the midst of trouble, thou wilt revive me" (Ps. 138:7, KJV).

- "My flesh and my heart faileth: but God is the strength of my heart" (Ps. 73:26, KJV).

- "The Lord upholdeth all that fall, and raiseth up all those that be bowed down" (Ps. 145:14, KJV).

Promise Fuels Realistic Hope

What practical help do promises afford us? Primarily, carrying promises such as these enable us to hear what

---

4   http://whatsaiththescripture.com/Promises/Clarkes_Bible_Promises.html

5   Eric W. Hayden, *Searchlight on Spurgeon: Spurgeon Speaks for Himself* (Pasadena, Texas: Pilgrim Publications, 1973), p. 178.

God's voice sounds like amid the torrent of competing voices that thrash the boarded up windows of our minds. We hear His strong and tender voice of love, presence, purpose and truth for us in Jesus. We lean by faith upon those promise words of our heavenly and tender Father, as Jesus did when the ancient fiend tempted Him in the wilderness. While the hissing serpent whispered thoughts to undo Him, the Savior responded, "It is written" (Matt. 4:1-11).

We, in the midst of dark forebodings, also run to the promise of what is written and to the presence of the One who wrote it. We hear there who God is, what is His posture toward us, and the larger story line of hope in which this current painful moment sits. Learning to recount God's promises as a way of life enables us to more readily hear the voice of our Shepherd amid the growl and fang of our wolves.

Sometimes God's promises ease our burden of mind. They "create in us an elevation of spirit, a life above visible surroundings, a calm and heavenly frame of mind."[6] They exist like soldiers of realistic hope who overtake our captors, cut the tapes and ropes that bind us, remove the blindfold, look us full in the eyes and tell us, "We've come to take you home."

Relief comes because promise fuels realistic hope. Such "hope, kindled by a divine promise, affects the entire life of a man in his inmost thoughts, ways, and feelings," Charles says.[7] Hope on the basis of promise swings open

---

6   Charles Spurgeon, *According to Promise* (Grace E-Books), p. 17 (http://grace-ebooks.com/library/Charles%20Spurgeon/CHS_According%20to%20Promise.PDF), accessed 4/4/14.

7   ibid., p. 16.

the curtains and lets the sunshine in again. At least if only for a minute, an hour, a day, a year, it is pleasant to see the sun.

At other times, promises spoken bring no felt relief at all. Like a toy fan in the desert, their batteries are dead. We clutch the toy fan while the heat drains our life away. In such times, Charles reminds us from experience that the effectiveness of God's promise does not depend upon our ability to feel it or see it. Just as the captive's hope for rescue depends not on her ability to recognize her rescuer or to reach out, but on the soldier's ability to remove what binds her and carry her to safety. The promise itself and the One who made it secure its anchor, even though at times we ourselves seem abandoned to the waves and tossed helplessly in our boats.

Because of God and His promise, realistic hope endures almost in secret, sometimes beneath the surfaces of our changing moods and miseries. Charles looks for this hope within a person despite their troubles. He points to this secret hope in comparison to whether or not one looks like a moral achiever on a given day. "The secret hope of a man is a truer test of his condition before God than the acts of any one day, or even the public devotions of a year."[8] A story larger and truer than our moods or miseries holds us. We are more than the trials, feelings or choices of a moment might suggest about us.

We Look for Like Cases in the Bible
We not only learn to write notes of God's promises to ourselves, we also become miners for promise within the caves of Scripture's pages. We go spelunking in the dark

---

8   ibid., p. 17.

amid the glimmer and dim of nightlights. Why do we look for promises in the Bible? Because God has given words of hope made applicable to meet "the innumerable varieties of his people's conditions. Not a single trial is overlooked, however peculiar it may be."[9]

What do we look for within these mines? We look for "the cases of other believers which are like our own ... the more exact the agreement" of our situation with theirs, "the greater the comfort which it will yield." When we find this kind of close situation to our own, we endeavor "to light upon that particular utterance of divine grace which is suitable to ourselves in our present circumstances."[10]

We avoid the dissonance. We know that we are not Moses or Hannah, Mary or Peter. Their tasks were unique. But we resonate with their common humanity, their common human emotions, thoughts, failings, trials and joys. We see how God related to them according to what is common with us. We trust that the character of God for them then will prove the same for us now.

So, we don't try to force ourselves into Bible stories. Just as a miner digs at a spot of promise only to find no treasure there, so we too embrace trial and error in our scripture mining. "You try one and another of the inspired words," Charles says, "but they do not fit."

> The troubled heart sees reasons to suspect that they are not strictly applicable to the case in hand, and so they are left in the old Book for use another day; for they are not available in the present emergency. You try again, and in due season a promise presents itself, which seems

---

9   Charles Spurgeon, *According to Promise*, p. 73.

10   ibid.

to have been made for the occasion; it fits as exactly as a well-made key fits the wards of the lock for which it was originally prepared.[11]

Let's pause for a moment to apply what Charles says here from the psalmist himself. Consider Psalm 77 as an example. Psalm 77 reveals a person despairing, sleepless, engulfed, whose thoughts about God only pain him more. He pours out his questions regarding the seeming absence of God within his miseries. But then this despairing psalmist begins to meditate on a story in the Scriptures he has learned. He meditates on the Israelites stalled with Moses, walled on one side by the sea and about to die on the other side at the hand of Pharaoh's armies. No way out presented itself. The depressed man then recounts the larger story of God to himself and for us on the basis of that previous story.

> Your way was through the sea,
>   your path through the great waters;
>   yet your footprints were unseen.
> You led your people like a flock
>   by the hand of Moses and Aaron. (Ps. 77:19-20)

The depressed man saw the dissonance between Moses' story and his. He did not believe that God promised to part an actual sea for him as a sign of presence and love. But the depressed man did behold the resonance of his own life story standing with those who generations before were trapped by the sea. The same God who delivered them through great waters with footprints unseen, could demonstrate that same heart, presence, and deliverance

---

11   ibid.

to him in his own trapped condition. The way forward for them was through. The psalmist takes up this truth for himself. God, though unseen, will lead him through his own stuck position. He took this as a pledge of God's character to get him through as well.

Charles' favorite mines to revisit for those with depression included Jacob's limp, Joseph's tears, Job's agonies, David's psalms, Elijah's desire to die, the laments of the Bible, Paul's thorn and, as we have seen, our Lord's misery in Gethsemane. But what is the point of finding such promises for our situations? Doesn't this just represent self-help sloganeering or trite affirmations for each day?

Pleading the Promises
Charles' answer is no. The promise isn't a bare word, but the word of God. To take up with it is to take up with Him. We help ourselves by appealing to them, but the help provided does not come from ourselves at all.

Rather, we live like those who've gone before us. We too can pray and cry out in relationship with God with our miseries. And this is the whole point of promise, that it leads us to prayer. We express personal relationship with God within the very moment of our gloom.

"What is prayer," Charles asks, "but the promise pleaded?" Then he tells us his own way of life regarding promise and prayer.

> I like in my time of trouble to find a promise which exactly fits my need, and then to put my finger on it, and say, "Lord, this is thy word; I beseech thee to prove that it is so, by carrying it out in my case. I believe that this is thine own writing; and I pray thee make it good to my faith." I believe in plenary inspiration, and I humbly look

to the Lord for a plenary fulfillment of every sentence that he has put on record.[12]

One promise that Charles repeatedly used for prayer was from Psalm 103:13: "As a father shows compassion to his children, so the Lord shows compassion to those who fear him." As with Jesus, who taught us to pray to God as our heavenly and loving Father, Charles remarked: "When we are lowest, we can still say, 'Our Father,' and when it is very dark, and we are very weak, our childlike appeal can go up, 'Father, help me! Father, rescue me!'"[13]

God says He is like a father who has compassion upon us in our weakness. So, we take Him at His word and plead this promise and prayer. We look for His compassion to manifest itself in the real moment of our plight.

Charles often retold a personal story about this pleading the promise of his being God's dearly loved child in Jesus. Wracked with extreme pain of body and mind related to gout, with no relief and no moment of respite, when he could no longer bear it without crying out, he cried to God on the basis of this promised pity in the Bible.

Thou art my Father, and I am Thy child; and Thou, as a Father, art tender and full of mercy. I could not bear to see my child suffer as Thou makest me suffer; and if I saw him tormented as I am now, I would do what I could to help him, and put my arms under him to sustain him. Wilt Thou hide Thy face from me, my Father? Wilt Thou still lay on me Thy heavy hand, and not give me a smile from Thy countenance?[14]

---

12 Charles Spurgeon, *According to Promise*, p. 42.

13 Charles Spurgeon, *C.H. Spurgeon's Autobiography 1856-1878*, p. 248. (http://books.google.com), accessed 4/4/14.

14 Charles Spurgeon, *C.H. Spurgeon's Autobiography 1856-1878*, p. 247.

In that instance, Charles was given an unexplainable relief so that he could rest. Those who saw him later noticed the marked change in that season of his health and countenance.

Pleading such promises and seeing answers to such pleadings can afford us reasons for gratitude and praise that we can recount to ourselves and call to strong remembrance when things go dark again. Such praises and testimonies of previous mercies shine upon the night seas, even should the fog veil their light. Veiled to us they yet shine in the remembrance of those who know us. They shine as testimonies of hope secured by the One who keeps us.

For this reason, Charles ached for those whose way of trying to cope did not include these promises of God. Yet, he was no trite promise-maker. He spoke of these medicines of promise as one who was never healed of his diseases of body and mind. From the night seas, he points us to the lamp piercing through his darkness and fog. In this, we learn the feisty faith of a broken man. We see the courage of one who hoped.

What Do We Learn?

(1) *Promises aren't magic.* They resemble love letters more than incantations, statements of truth more than immunity passes. They often forge, not a pathway for escape from life, but an enablement to endure what assails us.

(2) *Promises differ from our desires*, as tender and valued as our desires are to God. We earnestly pray our desires, particularly for our loved ones, because we know the merciful heart of God for us and for them. What we want and what God has promised are not always the same.

(3) *Promises must be Promises.* Not only must we distinguish our desires from God's promises, but we

also need help to make sure that what we lean upon is something that God has actually promised. For example, Charles did not believe that God promised to give us our desires for wealth, health, immunity from trial, pains or from dying in this life. What God has promised is to be with us, to weep with us, to celebrate with us, to help us, to strengthen us, to never let us go and to outlast every evil and terrible thing with us. His love, His purposes, and His goodness will never quit and no foul thing will ever overcome them. These kinds of "with us, for us, understands us, nothing can separate us" promises are like berries ripe and ready for our tasting. Health, wealth and immunity pledges are like wormed apples. They look good until you take a deeper bite.

(4) *Promises return us to Jesus.* In the man of sorrows, the cross and the victory of the empty tomb preach to us about the sufferer who is King. The promises of God are "yes and amen" in Him (2 Cor. 1:20). He will have the final word. He is the rescuer who regardless of our condition to adequately hold on, looks us in the eyes and says, "I've come for you. Home waits. Nothing will separate us again. Nothing."

10

Natural Helps

"We need patience under pain and hope under depression of spirit .... Our God ... will either make the burden lighter or the back stronger; he will diminish the need or increase the supply."[1]

We gathered together, standing in a circle, around the edges of the newly renovated room. Our tears and sniffles commemorated the young war veteran who violently ended his life in this same room one year earlier. One by one, friends, family and neighbors spoke thanks for their fallen friend.

For months, this room sat empty. No one ventured there. Pain and imagination overwhelmed and haunted the thought. After all, horrors took place there where the Bible

---

1   Charles Spurgeon, *Sword and Trowel* , January 1877 (Ages Digital Library, 1998), p. 15.

sat open on the table. Furniture and carpets were disfigured and carried off in the night while no one watched.

But now, a year later, the room was new again. Old memories met attempted hopes. We risked the room. We cried and we prayed.

The family had asked that I read from the Bible and offer a few words. A couple of minutes after I began, I heard someone giggle. I kept reading, and expounding, and another person giggled, then another. I became self-conscious. I solemnly kept reading. Then, as if helium balloons were let out of their holding bags, a whole gang of laughter burst forth into the room! Everyone was laughing but me with my Bible and solemn face. I stopped as someone apologized and sheepishly explained.

"Pastor, we are sorry. It's not you. (Small giggles and snorts.) Please keep reading. (More giggles and snorts.) You see, Jerry accidentally passed a little bit of gas a minute ago. (Lots of giggles and snorts.) And, well, the look on his face as he tried to stop it, and the look on your face as you read the Bible to us, well..."

By now, all of us burst into laughter together. Nothing more needed saying. We laughed and laughed. After a few moments, we gathered ourselves, blew our noses and held each other in our smiles. Soon enough I began to read again of the promises of God. Somehow the solemn had bloomed from the ground of terrible memory into the present air of human living. Laughter gave our tears room to breathe.

Laughter's Medicine
Over the many years of spending time in grief with people, I have noticed that laughter often glows intermittent amid

waves of tears, when friends gather, mourn together, and share stories. Have you noticed this too?

Charles quotes Proverbs 17:22, "A joyful heart is good medicine." He applies this wisdom, not just to grief, but to depression. "Cheerfulness readily carries burdens," he says, "which despondency dares not touch."[2]

This melancholy man seemed to pursue humor where he could find it. From being criticized for his humor in the pulpit to his collection of humorous anecdotes in his *John Ploughman Talks* and *Salt Cellar* writings, Charles' intentional pursuit of cheer where good cheer could be found is well described by his friend William Williams.

> What a bubbling fountain of humour Mr. Spurgeon had! I laughed more, I verily believe, when in his company than during all the rest of my life besides. He had the most fascinating gift of laughter … and he had also the greatest ability for making all who heard him laugh with him.[3]

One of Charles' early biographers compared him to Abraham Lincoln because of their common melancholy and pensiveness of mood.[4] These two brave men shared another commonality. They shared a way of doing life in which good humor was sought out and collected in order to give vent for their moods and gloom.[5] We, too, can

---

2   Charles Spurgeon, "Bells for the Horses," *MTP* (http://www.spurgeon. org/s_and_t/bells.htm), accessed 3/19/14.

3   Larry J. Michael, "The Medicine of Laughter: Spurgeon's Humor," (http:// www.InternetEvangelismDay.com/medicine.php#ixzz2wRAfObT2), accessed 3/19/14.

4   Justin D. Fulton, *Charles H. Spurgeon: Our Ally* (Philadephia: H.J. Smith & Co., 1892), p. 256.

5   Shenk, *Lincoln's Melancholy*, p. 113.

become a daily collector of cheerful stories and anecdotes to vent our gloom. Though death invade our room, laughter and human welcome need not flee. In time, even after the worst frost and cold, spring still comes.

In addition to promises and prayers and the gracious aid of the man of sorrows, sufferers of depression, whether seasonal or chronic, can seek a way of life that calms rather than agitates their glooms. The same Savior that holds us also provides a collection of helps for our use. In addition to ordinary humor, Charles summarizes this collection of helps. "Beyond all medicine, stimulant, cordial, or lecturing," he says, "I commend quiet hours in calm retreats."[6]

Let's look at these helps and their invitation to reshaping how we do a day. Let's start first with his commendation of "quiet hours and calm retreats."

Quiet Hours and Calm Retreats

In 1879, against his own wishes, Charles was compelled to take a furlough for three months. Those who communicated on his behalf described all the "demands made upon head and heart" that made the strain too great. Charles' "mind and spirit" sank "into painful depression," from which there was "no recovery but by rest."[7] He found extended rest in Mentone, France.

Over the years, though he often resisted the fact that he had to do it, Charles built into his life annual seasons of winter removal into this land of sunshine and flowers.

---

6   Charles Spurgeon, "Bells for the Horses," in *Sword and Trowel* (http://www.spurgeon.org/s_and_t/bells.htm), accessed 3/14/14.

7   Charles Spurgeon, *Sword and Trowel 1879* (Ages Digital Library, 1998), p. 522.

"Communion with nature," as he called it, eased the gloom and fatigue which the fog, frost, and damp of London agitated amid the pain of work. The cold wet days of winter acted upon his "sensitive frame" like "the atmosphere operates on a barometer. Dull and dreary days depressed him."[8]

Psychologists at the time commended this practice: "the removal of a patient from the cares of business, or from family anxieties, surrounding him, in a cheerful country residence, with new scenes, new faces, new objects of attention, and subjects for thought."[9]

Charles also began to surrender to his limits with work such as saying "no" to extra travel and speaking opportunities, though this was a struggle for him.

> The choice seems to lie between being laid aside pretty frequently with depression of spirit and pain of body, and steadily keeping on with home duties; we prefer the second, because we hope that the comparative quiet may bring greater strength for future endeavors.[10]

Trying to find a routine of nature and rest did not promote workless days. In fact, Charles' work output explains a lot about his help to others, his reminder that our infirmity does not diminish our contribution and, negatively, his regular need to stop. The point is his wrestling match with these routines formed a different way of work. The more

---

8   Charles Spurgeon, *Autobiography Vol. 4* (http://www.grace-ebooks. com/library/Charles%20Spurgeon/CHS_Autobiography/CHS_ Autobiography%20Vol%204.PDF), p. 362. accessed 3/17/14.

9   Bucknill, *A Manual of Psychological Medicine*, p. 500.

10   Charles Spurgeon, *Sword and Trowel*, July 1877 (Ages Digital Library, 1998), p. 161.

he could embrace these routines, the better it suited his pain of mind and body.

In this light, Charles often taught, wrote, met with visitors and counseled people while in Mentone; but not always and in dramatically more limited fashion. In a generation, in which the medicines that existed were crude and less helpful, Charles chiefly commended nature and rest as a way of healing. What does this mean for those who suffer and those who do life with the suffering?

1. *Find ways to make contact with nature and sunshine.* This is the "best medicine for hypochondriacs, the surest tonics for the declining, the best refreshments for the weary."[11]

2. *Become intentional about seasonal rhythms:* Pay attention to how weather, work and rest function for your gloom. "Rest is the best, if not the only medicine for those occupied with mental pursuits and subject to frequent depression of spirit." In that light, "Get away, ye sons of sadness, from your ordinary avocations for a little season if you possibly can and enjoy quiet and repose."[12] The congregation in London learned to accept this limit of their pastor's humanity and to embrace it as part of his fruitful life and ministry.

3. *Meanwhile, limit your work to what you can do healthily and break up your day into smaller portions.* "The very best thing in the world, when you are nervous and

---

11 Charles Spurgeon, *Lectures to My Students*, p. 177.

12 Charles Spurgeon, "A Sermon for the Most Miserable of Men," *MTP*, Vol. 15 (Ages Digital Library, 1998), p. 80.

troubled, is to live by very short periods ... live by the day; or, better still, live moment by moment."[13]

It pains us and those who do life with us sometimes, but we sufferers cannot keep up with the speed that efficiency and others require of us, at least not for long. We take longer and go slower, with everything, strategically so for our strength. But this pace makes manageable what otherwise isn't, and will produce fruit that we otherwise cannot. The melancholy life thrives when it marathons instead of sprints, or when it sprints often, only to rest often. You needn't try to do "the most things" in "the fastest ways" anymore. To resist this is to have seasons of rest and nature forced upon us by breakdown.

Medicines

Nature and rest aren't the only medicines. The drugs of depression have names like, "Elavil, Ludiomil, Doxepin, Norpramin, Prozac, Lithium, Xanax, Wellbutrin, Parnate, Nardil, Zoloft,"[14] Lexapro or Ritilan.

In Charles' lifetime, pharmaceuticals for melancholia also existed. These drugs had names too: Tartrate of Antimony, Calomel, Morphia, Opium and Laudanum. What Charles took for his depression, if anything, is unknown to me. He normatively spoke of opiates or laudanum as a metaphor for negative and detrimental aspects in the spiritual life. But what we know for sure is that when Charles mentions medicine he helps us in our fellow sufferings in at least three ways.

---

13   Charles Spurgeon, "The Saddest Cry from the Cross," *MTP*, Vol. 48 (Ages Digital Library, 1998), p. 663.

14   Kenyon, p. 232.

First, taking medicine is a wise act of faith, not of unfaith. "It would not be wise to live by a supposed faith, and cast off the physician and his medicines, any more than to discharge the butcher, and the tailor, and expect to be fed and clothed by faith," he said. "We make use of medicines, but these can do nothing apart from the Lord, 'who healeth all our diseases.'"[15] Likewise, when appealing to James 5:14-15, Charles observes, "Certainly, when the Holy Spirit spoke concerning sick men," He "advised that medicines should be used, and prayer for their restoration."[16]

Second, Charles himself took medicines and pills.[17] "Have you never noticed that some people who are ill and are ordered to take pills are foolish enough to chew them?" Charles asks. "That is a very nauseous thing to do, though I have done it myself."[18]

Third, he believed that medicine in itself was not enough. Prayer, nature, rest, stimulants, cordials and lectures also remained necessary. Psychological theory at the time likewise assumed that drugs could help, but not act alone in treating most cases.

Instead, in addition to medicinal treatment, a patient also required "hygienic" and "moral" helps. "Hygienic" helps included warm baths, cold compresses, removal to the countryside, and uninterrupted sleep. Moral helps

15   Charles Spurgeon, "Beloved, and Yet Afflicted," Sermon 1518 (http://www.spurgeon.org/sermons/1518.htm), accessed 3/14/14.

16   Charles Spurgeon, "The Oil of Gladness," Sermon 1273 (http://www.spurgeon.org/sermons/1273.htm), accessed 3/14/14.

17   Spurgeon, *Autobiography*, p. 369.

18   Charles Spurgeon, "Salvation by Knowing the Truth," *MTP*, Sermon 1516 (http://www.spurgeon.org/sermons/1516.htm), accessed 3/19/14.

included what we'd today refer to as therapy and pastoral care. The experience of most sufferers evidenced this need for multiple treatment approaches.[19]

Today, medications have advanced dramatically. But while these drugs offer substantial help, some longtime sufferers of depression can tire of feeling chained to drugs for years. Or they find help but in such a way that aspects of their personality, which they value, get numbed or rendered ineffective. Others declare that medication doesn't seem to help them at all.[20] In sum, medication for our bodily and mental illnesses is an aid and gift, but even our best medications remain limited. Medicines help us, but rarely in isolation from other helps.

Consequently, Charles spoke often of other kinds of "medicines" in addition to pharmaceuticals that we ought not to overlook.

Stimulants, Cordials, (Diet) and Lectures

The *Manual of Psychological Medicine 1858* recognizes help for melancholy in the form of stimulants such as Port Wine or Egg Flip (a warm Egg Nog mixed with Ale and Rum).[21] Similarly, a Cordial referred at the time to a syrup or drink usually, but not always containing some type of alcohol or opiate. At a time in which leeches were still placed on the human scalp, and in which bleeding with a lancet was still used (albeit controversially), medicines, rest, and diet were supplemented by the strategic use of alcohol.

---

19 John Charles Bucknill and Daniel Hack Tuke, *A Manual of Psychological Medicine* (London, 1858), p. 498. (https://archive.org/stream/manualofp sycholo00buckrich#page/162/mode/2up), accessed 3/12/14.

20 Shenk, *Unholy Ghost*, p. 254.

21 *Manual of Psychological Medicine 1858,* pp. 532-33.

This aspect of Charles' life has roused continual controversy. Desirous to prove that Charles abstained from alcohol, some point to his support of the temperance movement, along with his use of juice at the communion table. Others point to his early years of drink. Add to this his use of cigars as a stimulant, and the reader understands why at this exact moment someone is ready to parse my every word and decide the merits of this book by the next sentences I write.

This subject also tempts us. Many who struggle with the terrible miseries of depression often turn to intoxication from drugs or alcohol as a way to numb the pain. For a while, this numbing helps. But over time, the addition of addiction to depression only increases the difficulty and the struggle. The shame of depression has to soon share the bed with the shame of addiction. No wonder, the weight becomes too heavy and the bed becomes like a chain, which keeps us bound.

Given the amount of physical and mental misery, which Charles experienced amid the context of crude medical helps, appropriate uses of stimulants and cordials offer no surprise.

- *In contrast to opiates and laudanum, which he used only in negative terms, Charles regularly used stimulants and cordials as metaphors to describe positive aspects of the Christian life such as reviving and encouraging.* The word stimulant or cordial therefore did not intrinsically offend his Baptist hearers at the time or himself. Types of stimulants and cordials existed which were acceptable and viewed positively.

- *Charles made use of medicinal stimulants prescribed by doctors.* In 1892, Charles' brother James writes: "I can assure you that my dear brother was and remained up to his death an abstainer from strong beverages of an intoxicating character. Medicinally I have no doubt he may have had given him some form of a stimulant and then he would under such circumstances take any drug so prescribed but otherwise he never took anything of the form or kind in any shape. Whoever says he did speaks wrongly."[22] Charles did not choose alcohol or drunkenness as his way of coping. Many have and have been stung by the emptiness of it, though for a time it numbed their pain, it robbed them of other joys. In contrast, the accountable and medicinal use of measured stimulants proved an aid to Charles and can in like fashion do so for us.

- *Before he eventually quit the practice, Charles made use of cigars in similar fashion.* "When I have found intense pain relieved, a weary brain soothed, and calm, refreshing sleep obtained by a cigar, I have felt grateful to God, and have blessed His name."[23]

- *Charles also made use of warm baths as a stimulant. The Manual of Psychological Medicine* prescribed warm baths with cold compresses for the head. Charles utilized this kind of hydrophatic bath.[24] Daily or timely warm baths placed into our routine can prove helpful for some.

- *Attention to food and fasting also formed medicinal help for Charles' pains.*[25] Food has its own impact on our

---

22 Fulton, *Charles H. Spurgeon: Our Ally*, p. 263.

23 Charles Spurgeon, Personal Letter to the *Daily Telegraph,* September 23, 1874 (http://www.spurgeon.org/misc/cigars.htm), accessed 3/12/14.

24 Spurgeon, *Autobiography*, (http://www.cblibrary.org/biography/spurgeon/spurg_v2/spau2_18.htm), accessed 3/19/14.

25 Spurgeon, *Autobiography*, p. 369.

minds and bodies. Attention to its role in our mental anxieties is worthwhile.

Added to nature, rest, medicine, laughter, prescribed stimulants and baths, Charles also mentioned the benefit of lectures as a help for our suffering. Lectures refer to instruction and talk. Therapy, pastoral care, sermons, teaching, education and conversation, these verbal helps matter. Most of this book to this point has focused on this aspect of what we say or need to hear regarding depression in its various forms.

But even sermons, workshops and counseling sessions have their limits. "Sick men want more than instruction," Charles reminds us, "they require our cordials (by which he means encouragement) and supports."[26] Without this recognition of multiple helps, even psychologists of the time concurred: "a clergyman may be a learned theologian but powerless as a pastor."[27] If we offer only prayer and sermon to aid the mental suffering of our neighbors, we underestimate the body-soul need and the many gifts in nature that God has mercifully provided.

The Savior through whom our souls find aid, is the same One through whom all things were created. The natural aids of His creation join with promises and prayer to forge a preferred way of routine and life, conducive for our strength.

The Carlini Effect

In his sermon, *A Sacred Solo*, Charles recounts the story of a man who sought a physician. He hoped the physician

---

26 Charles Spurgeon, "The Glorious Master and the Swooning Desciple," Sermon 1028, *MTP* (http://www.spurgeon.org/sermons/1028.htm), accessed 3/14/14.

27 *Manual of Psychological Medicine 1858*, p. 548.

would prescribe medicine to help his lowness of spirits and habitual despondency. The physician did provide medicine but also suggested that he go to the theater to hear Carlini, whose humor, fun and frolic were renowned. "If Carlini can't fetch the blues of you, nobody will!" the doctor exclaimed. "Alas! Sir," said the patient, "I am Carlini."[28]

Medicines, good humor, rest, nature, baths, diet, scheduling our days according to our limits, therapy and pastoral counsel, each of these is given for our aid and offer us great help. We learn to alter and reorient our days around the use of these good gifts. Charles struggled and resisted these at times. At other times, his overwork and inadequate rest and diet forced him to depend upon such helps.

These helps cannot stand alone though. He knew that. These helps need each other and they also depend upon the "man of sorrows." Charles knew that too and so, now, do we. The ordinary gifts we often overlook become now the very helps on which we depend. We are not ashamed. We are wise. We are not slow and behind. We are finding a capacity for meaning, beauty, depth and reality that few who are clear-brained ever stop to learn.

---

28 Charles Spurgeon, "A Sacred Solo," *MTP*, Vol. 24 (Ages Digital Library, 1998), p. 498.

11

Suicide and Choosing Life

"I wonder every day that there are not more suicides, considering the troubles of this life."[1]

Sometimes despondency rejects our sense of God's help. Solid reasons for hope exist in the "man of sorrows," but "alas, when under deep depression the mind forgets all this, and is only conscious of its unutterable misery."[2] Sermons prove hard to bear. The friend who quotes verses feels like one who shouts at the migrained. Promises and prayers fade. Rest, medicine, baths, humor or talk grow empty.

---

1   Charles Spurgeon, "Chastisement," *NPSP*, Sermon 48, *The Spurgeon Archive* (http://www.spurgeon.org/sermons/0048.htm), accessed 12/13/13.

2   Spurgeon, "Israel's God and God's Israel," *MTP*, Vol. 14 p. 238.

Conscious only of our miseries, we become like those who love a person without that love being returned. To carry out the metaphor, what is worse, we must listen in as the one we love marries another and goes on with life happily without us. We receive the wedding invitation and try to attend. But all of their love talk and intimacies, the toasts and cheers from their family and friends, only magnifies the absence, anxiety and rejection with which we must live. This is what it is like with God. We take up the language given to us by the Psalmist, "When I remember God, I moan: when I meditate, my spirit faints. Selah" (Ps. 77:3).

"There are times," therefore, "when all our evidences" regarding God "get clouded, and all our joys are fled. Though we may still cling to the cross, yet it is with a desperate grasp."[3]

The Desire to Die

May I say it plainly? Sometimes in our depression we, or those we love, want to die. No amount of promises or prayers, medicines or warm baths can make us immune to this desire. Like the man of sorrows we are worn thin and tired. But unlike him, we lose sight of the joy set before us. We can no longer hold on to the larger story and yet we remain fully conscious of an accumulation of anguishes. We let go of hope. Or we choose to hope in death or in Jesus beyond the grave. We who remain wail in shock and loss.

Charles knew this desire for death. He found language for it in the story of Job whose profound description of misery not only reveals why in our afflictions of body and mind we would want to die but also the manifest mercy of God who would inspire such grief words and call them scripture.

---

3   Spurgeon, "The Frail Leaf," p. 590.

I am allotted months of emptiness,
and nights of misery are apportioned to me.
When I lie down I say, "When shall I arise?"
But the night is long,
and I am full of tossing till the dawn.
My flesh is clothed with worms and dirt;
my skin hardens, then breaks out afresh.
My days are swifter than a weaver's shuttle
and come to their end without hope ...
my eye will never again see good ...
When I say, "My bed will comfort me,
my couch will ease my complaint,"
then you scare me with dreams
and terrify me with visions,
so that I would choose strangling
and death rather than my bones.
I loathe my life ...
What is man, that you ...
visit him every morning
and test him every moment?
How long will you not look away from me,
nor leave me alone till I swallow my spit? (Job 7:13-19)

Charles draws upon these sacred words of anguish. He applies them to himself so that those who want to die will find in their preacher one who understands. I too "could say with Job, 'My soul chooseth strangling rather than life,'" Charles testified. "I could readily enough have laid violent hands upon myself, to escape from my misery."[4]

In fact, Charles makes clear that he has felt this desire more than once. When referring to Elijah's prayer to die in 1 Kings 19:4, Charles refers to his own experience by

---

4   Charles Spurgeon, "The Shank-Bone Sermon; Or, True Believers and their Helpers," *MTP*, Vol. 36 (Ages Digital Library, 1998), p. 252.

saying, "I know one who, in the bitterness of his soul, has often prayed it."[5]

Affirming the Sanity of Wanting to Die

Charles tells us of his own desires to die with hope so that we will be helped to learn that we are not alone in this experience. He goes even further to affirm that miseries worse than death exist in this world and in our lives. Turning to Psalm 88, which describes what we feel when darkness has become our only companion, Charles declares that a misery "worse than physical death has cast its dreadful shadow over us." In such cases, he recognizes that "death would be welcomed as a relief by those whose depressed spirits make their existence a living death."[6]

Charles further highlights this feeling that death is a lesser pain by looking to Jesus, when our Lord uttered the words, "My soul is exceedingly sorrowful even unto death" (Matt. 26:38, KJV). In this scene, Charles finds further testimony and description of why death offers relief. We are so weak that we barely recognize that we are actually living. We feel as if we are "scarcely alive." We wish that we could become unconscious because the consciousness we possess is so extremely painful.[7]

In other words, Charles approached our desire to die in our sufferings, not with distant critique or calloused faith-checking, but with depth and affirmation. Why? To understand and to be understood.

---

5   Charles Spurgeon, "Elijah Fainting," *MTP*, Vol. 47 (Ages Digital Library, 1998), p. 273.

6   Charles Spurgeon, Psalm 88, *Treasury of David, The Spurgeon Archive* http://www.spurgeon.org/treasury/ps088.htm, accessed 12/13/13.

7   ibid.

Reminding us of Elijah for example, Charles answers by saying, "It was the most rational thing in the world for Elijah to be sick at heart and to desire to die."[8] His miseries were not illusory but real. His wish for death did not reveal his insanity but demonstrated the opposite. "A desire to depart when it arises from wisdom and knowledge and from a general survey of things below is very proper,"[9] Charles suggests.

Likewise when Job asks God, "Wilt thou break a leaf driven to and fro?" Charles advocates for the afflicted and affirms the reasonableness of the question. Those "stricken with disease, stung with smart and fretted with acute pains and pangs," can understandably feel that if their "affliction continued much longer, it were better for them to die than live."[10]

We've already noted the irrationalities ignited by depression. Imaginary terrors, frightful memories, presumed tragedies that never come to pass, can harass our thoughts like the tree outside our window, which we mistook for a stalker peeking in. Yet, Charles reminds us that the anguish itself, even when caused by imaginary woes, remains real. "Some people are excessively nervous: they are afraid the skies will fall or the earth will crack." Of course such thoughts are irrational. "But the agony caused thereby is very real. There is little of the Christian spirit in the man who can increase mental torment by turning it into jest."[11]

This desire for death among the afflicted confronts us with mysteries we cannot fathom and we loved ones want

8   Spurgeon, "Faintness and Refreshing," p. 588.

9   ibid., p. 586.

10   Spurgeon, "The Frail Leaf," p. 589.

11   Spurgeon, "Helps to Full Assurance," p. 516.

no part of. "It might puzzle us to tell why Elijah should get under a juniper bush," Charles acknowledges. "But when we get under the juniper ourselves, we are glad to recall the fact that Elijah once sat there," he continues. "When we are hiding away in the cave, it is a source of comfort to us to remember that such a man as this great prophet of Israel was there before us."[12]

Therefore, the mercy of God in the Scriptures asserts itself again. "The experience of one saint" described on the sacred pages "is instructive to others."[13] Even "saints" can desire to die. We too can say in the midst of all that grieves us, "I hated life" (Eccles. 2:17) and with Job, Jeremiah and Solomon we too can feel that it were better had we never been born.

Some of us at this moment can put this book down for a moment. We can pause, weep, and pray with empathy for how miserable the howling abyss must be that can lead a human being to desire to end his or her life. And how courageous an act of faith it must require of them to choose otherwise day by day. How strong and merciful are the arms of grace to hold our collapsing selves on a given day.

Therefore, be careful that your fears do not keep you from listening as a caregiver or your certainties keep you from talking as a sufferer. "It is often a wonderful relief to be able to tell out your grief." The hymn writer who wrote, "Bear and forebear, and silent be; Tell no man thy misery," was mistaken, Charles says. On the contrary, "it is a very sweet thing to unburden your heart."[14]

---

12   Spurgeon, "Elijah Fainting," 272.

13   ibid.

14   ibid., 281.

Exposing the Folly of Wanting to Die

Up to this point, though it frightens us as loved ones and hopefully vindicates us who suffer, we've acknowledged the fact of death wishes in our lives. But now, the problem we have is not ultimately this desire for death but the illusions and supposed remedies which we choose to satisfy this desire. "When a wish to die is merely the result of passion, a sort of quarreling with God as a child sometimes quarrels with its parents," Charles teaches, "it has more of folly in it than of wisdom, and much more of petulance than of piety."[15]

When Jesus and the larger story of the gospel are eclipsed, we suicidal wishers, for all of our self-condemnation, unwittingly exalt ourselves to a high place of knowledge and importance. In that state, we assume an all-knowing posture; declaring that all possible and future goods have died for us. Our misery has poisoned us with a tragic arrogance. Our pains have deluded our reasoning. From our god-like vantage point, we tragically and misguidedly declare to ourselves and to others, "my eye will never again see good." An all-or-nothing misinformation infiltrates our convictions.

In messages such as *Paul's Desire to Depart*[16] Charles identifies the tragedy of these all-or-nothing convictions that drown us in selfishness. These messages deny the present and future power of Jesus.

- Circumstances are always hard. Life will only be bad always.

---

15   Spurgeon, "Faintness and Refreshing," 586.

16   Charles Spurgeon, "Paul's Desire to Depart," *NPSP*, Sermon 274 (http://www.spurgeon.org/sermons/0274.htm), accessed 4/5/14.

- People are terrible. People will never change and will always do wrong.

- I'm disappointed. I lost. Without him, her or it, I'm nothing. I can't live without them or it or with this failure.

- I'm embarrassed. I can't live with others mocking my shame.

- I'm mistreated and always will be. I will never be the same.

- I'm old and set in my ways. Nothing new could happen to me.

- I didn't get what I wanted. If I can't have it my way there is no point. I will have it my way or no way.

- I'm guilty. I've done terrible things. I can never recover from the wrong I've done.

Why We Are Meant to Choose Life

In response to these all-or-nothing declarations about our certain future gloom, Charles counters by quoting 1 Corinthians 2:9 as a promise beneath whose shade we can rest: "Eye hath not seen, nor ear heard, neither have entered into the heart of man, the things which God hath prepared for them that love him" (KJV). This inability to know the future applies to both kinds of death wishes.

First, speaking to the one who wants to die in order to be with Jesus, Charles reminds Christians that we know the rest of Elijah's story. If Elijah had known then every moment of meaning that still awaited him on Horeb, or on behalf of Naboth, or with Elisha, or for the school of the prophets, or the wondrous irony of a chariot of fire, Elijah would have wanted to live till they occurred.

And so it is with us. "You do not know, brother, how much there is for you yet to live for; and you, my sister, do not talk about dying; for you also have a great deal more to do," Charles urges. "You will be like men that dream; and your mouth shall be filled with laughter, and your tongue with singing, and you will say, 'The Lord hath done great things for us.'"[17]

In other words, when Elijah said, "It is enough, now, O Lord, take away my life," he was mistaken in his judgment. "It wasn't enough." He was wrong. His pain was lying to him regarding his ability to know his future, and his future in truth was filled with blessing.

We are reminded of wonderful mercy. People like Job, Moses, Elijah, and Jonah expressed their desire to die fully and without holding back. But they left the answer to their desires with God. They asked God to decide their lives, and refrained from deciding for themselves. How hard that must have been, harder than most can fathom.

Yet, sometimes the most courageous acts of faith and wisdom look like a human being mentally harassed and wanting to die, collapsed and held before the throne of grace. "Others think you foolish, call you nervous, and bid you rally yourself, but they know not your case. Did they understand it they would not mock you with such admonitions."[18]

Second, Charles spoke not only to Christians but also to those who wanted to die for reasons other than Jesus. He appeals first to testimony. The Apostle Paul experienced nearly every bullet point on our list of suicide messages noted above. Terrible circumstances, enemies,

---

17   Spurgeon, "Elijah Fainting," p. 284.

18   Charles Spurgeon, "The Agony in Gethsemane," *MTP*, Vol. 20 (Ages Digital Library, 1998), p. 739.

disappointment, embarrassment, mistreatment, suffering, old age, and guilt from terrible things forged the storyline of his life. Yet, in Jesus, Paul found a new identity, a new life. He found that he could live without the treasures and esteem that he once thought necessary. He discovered that he could live with embarrassments, slanders, shaming and mistreatments that he once thought unbearable. Forgiveness had forged a way for a good life; a life different from what he once thought he had to have, but better.

Paul received this grace from Jesus. Jesus was made the brunt of disappointments, terrible circumstances, relentless mistreatments, and having a guilt that was not His own placed upon Him. But those who were harassed and helpless, restless and lost, despairing and brain spooked, found love and healing in Him unlike they had ever known. The garden in which depression engulfed Him; the cross on which He bodily suffered, the death over which He triumphed, the intercession that He now invites you to, brings realistic hope to the proximity of your despair and mine.

For this reason, Charles also pled with those who were not saved by this grace of Jesus to by all means resist the temptation to kill one's self. Without this Savior waiting on the other side, suicide was like a bait hiding its hook. Far from helping or relieving one's plight, such a death only increased the proximity of despair. And this time, no hope, realistic or otherwise, can be found.

What Do We Learn?

1. *The truest Christians can experience depression and desire death.* "We are the strangest mixture of contra-dictions that ever was known," Charles says. "We shall

never be able to understand ourselves." Doubts can hound the faithful.[19]

2. *The truest Christians can do foolish things.* For a courageous believer to quiver toward death "is strange; but we are very strange creatures. There is not a man here who is not foolish at times; certainly, he who is in the pulpit takes precedence of you all in that respect."[20]

3. *We must take great care before judging someone who tries to overcome miseries that we ourselves have never encountered.* "We only need to be driven up into a corner, as Elijah was, and our folly will be discovered as was his; he ought to have prayed to live, yet he prayed that he might die."[21] "In the time of testing, you also will be as weak as other men."[22]

4. *The doubting Christian is not God-forsaken.* "Nobody doubts that Elijah was a child of God; nobody questions the fact that God loved him even when he sat fainting under the juniper tree." Even if we and Elijah have "cherished passions" under that tree of which God "does not approve," "The Lord did not forsake Elijah and he will not forsake you."[23]

5. We are what we are by the grace of God. This scene reminds us that "Elijah was not strong by nature, but only in the strength imparted to him by God; so that when the divine strength was gone, he was of no more

---

19   Spurgeon, "Sweet Stimulants for the Fainting Soul," p. 578.

20   Spurgeon, "Elijah Fainting," p. 278.

21   ibid.

22   ibid., p. 275.

23   ibid., p. 273.

account than anybody else."[24] "He failed as all God's people do; I scarcely know of any exception in all the biographies of the Old or New Testament."[25]

Rebuilding Our Hope

Suicide is not the unpardonable sin. The follower of Jesus is not lost, because of this heinous act. This gives us who remain hope for those we've loved.

And yet, the sad consequences remain, not only for those who chose suicide but for those left behind who loved them. Just as other sins are paid for by Christ, so this one is too. But just as other sins damage ourselves and others, this one is no exception.

We forfeit the future we could have known. We inflict terrible harm on those who love us and whom we loved. We give ourselves over to the very things that Jesus died to save us from. Forgiven and home with Him, yes! Yes! But much that must be paid for by Jesus and healed.

We loved ones who remain are forced into imaginations and memories forever scarred by gruesome scenes. Loss of love, time, gift, and meaning break our hearts and change us. We may become more angry or harder than we once were. We may become sleepless or more melancholy than we once were. We too will need help to forgive the selfish choice. We too may even face the temptation to copycat the suicide and inflict double harm on the community. And, if our loved one disbelieved in Jesus, we ache with terrible imaginations of heaven's absence for them. We wrestle toward hope in the mercy of God upon persons and choices that we can't control. We labor to imagine the

---

24   Spurgeon, "Elijah Fainting," p. 273.

25   ibid.

presence of His mercy in the last violent moment rousing our loved one to cry out and lean upon Him. In all of these imaginings we suffer the unknown.

Hope has been dismantled, maybe for all intents and purposes destroyed. But a larger story exists in Jesus. In time, even hope demolished can become hope rebuilt, if it is realistic and rooted, not just in the cross and empty tomb but also in the garden and the sweat-like blood.

In the meantime, Charles' comment and prayer become our own:

> Death would be welcomed as a relief by those whose depressed spirits make their existence a living death. Are good men ever permitted to suffer thus? Indeed they are; and some of them are even all their lifetime subject to bondage. O Lord, Be pleased to set free thy prisoners of hope! Let, none of thy mourners imagine that a strange thing has happened unto him, but rather rejoice as he sees the footprints of brethren who have trodden this desert before.[26]

---

26   Spurgeon, *Treasury Psalm 88*.

12

The Benefits of Sorrow

"To be cast down is often the best thing that could happen to us."[1]

It is rarely wise and often unkind to say what Charles says in this quotation, during the first moments of a crisis, while someone vomits from chemo, showers off from bodily assault, absorbs the loss of their job, or weeps by the graveside of their child. In such moments, we learn from the best practice of Job's friends. We say nothing. We sit in the ashes. We weep with those who weep. We talk more to God about them than we talk to them about God.

---

1   Charles Spurgeon, "Sweet Stimulants for the Fainting Soul," *MTP*, Vol. 48 (Ages Digital Library, 1998), p. 581.

We need not declare in these early horrid moments the difference grace and time in God's hands can make. We wisely say nothing.

Some within the Psychological community of Charles' day understood this too. Often, before we can offer "moral" helps to the suffering, we must first clear the way by allowing time, care without speech, and other hygienic and medicinal helps to lessen the anxieties and moods of the present trauma. As pain lessens and clarity recovers, bits of cracker and ice can be swallowed without throwing them back up. Sentences and silences can slowly gather into conversation and, sooner or later, together we will talk of God and His purpose for all of this.

Then, we will get back to it and ask the ancient question together one more time. Whether we believe in God or prefer to believe our doubts about Him, this ancient question remains the same. In common with the entire history of humanity, what we sufferers want to know is "Why?"

Staring into Bedlam

It isn't that we have nothing to go on. We can describe a lot about the "what" of sorrows in their various forms, including the very worst of mental disorders. Charles, for example, pastored his church just down the street from Saint Luke's Hospital. He describes the "what" that he saw when walking down its hallways; "Broken bones, disorders that depress the system, maladies incurable, pangs that rack and convulse the frame, and pains all but unbearable."[2]

---

2   Charles Spurgeon, "Overwhelming Obligations," *MTP*, Vol. 16 (Ages Digital Library, 1998), p. 33.

Also just down the street, Charles tells us that there "stands a dome" not far from the spot on which he presently speaks. Charles' voice then noticeably sobers. "I thank God for the existence of the place of which it forms a part—but I can never look at it," he says. Then, perhaps thinking back to when his own mind tottered on the brink, Charles pauses and says, "I hope I never shall look at it, without lifting up my heart in thanks to God that my reason is spared."[3] The dome Charles refers to is Bethlehem Hospital, or as we know it today, Bedlam.

Then, he imagines Bedlam's hallways. With empathy and mystery he goes on to describe the "what" of our broken minds. "It is no small unhappiness to be bereft of our faculties, to have the mind swept to and fro in hurricanes of desperate raging madness, or to be victims of hallucinations that shut you out from all usefulness, and even companionship with your fellow man."[4]

Bedlam causes Charles to speak of "those who have suffered the entire loss of their reason." But he admits that "no practical result" will flow from trying to understand how God and His grace explain a human being in this terrible condition. "So, I leave it alone," he says.[5]

At this, the preacher disappoints us who want an answer. The man of God is human too. He doesn't know and neither do we. We only know "what" to describe, but not why, if God is God, He allows such suffering.

---

3   Charles Spurgeon, "Overwhelming Obligations," *MTP*, Vol. 16, p. 33.

4   ibid.

5   Charles Spurgeon, "A Promise for the Blind," *MTP*, vol. 55 (Ages Digital Library, 1998), p. 233.

I Would Not Change It

We also know a lot about "how" sorrows and depression in their various forms work in our lives. In this book, we've described the miseries of them. But surprising benefits to sorrow also forge part of what we know.

After all, sometimes sufferers say a strange thing. They give thanks for what they've suffered. Not everyone of course. We know full well how sorrows can negatively change a person – they can harden us, embitter us, shatter our faith in God and make us cynical about people.

But many who wish that their suffering didn't happen nonetheless tell us that they have come to learn good things, which they otherwise would not. Charles is one such person. "I often feel very grateful to God that I have undergone fearful depression," he declares. "I know the borders of despair and the horrible brink of that gulf of darkness into which my feet have almost gone."[6]

But why is he grateful for depression? He answers, "Hundreds of times I have been able to give a helpful grip to brethren and sisters who have come into that same condition, which grip I could never have given if I had not known their deep despondency."[7] Not all of us are ready to say what Charles is saying. Our pain runs too deep.

But it can help us to know that Charles did not express this gratitude for depression tritely. At times, he could meditate on the same subject and come to a different conclusion. "I have never heard yet of anybody who derived any good from despair."[8] He also couldn't be trite

---

6   Charles Spurgeon, *The Soul Winner* (http://www.spurgeon.org/misc/sw14.htm), accessed 3/21/14.

7   ibid.

8   Charles Spurgeon, "A Discourse to the Despairing," (http://www.spurgeongems.org/vols40-42/chs2379.pdf), accessed 3/21/14.

because his transparency about depression cost him. Some even used his depression against him as a means to dismiss what he had to say.[9]

Yet, amid the painful ebb and flow of these sufferings, Charles repeatedly returned to the conviction that he would not trade his faith or his sufferings. We too might in time find our way down this surprising path.

> I have suffered as much bodily pain as most here present, and I know also about as much of depression of spirit at times as anyone.... I would not change with the most healthy man, or the most wealthy man, or the most learned man, or the most eminent man in all the world, if I had to give up my faith in Jesus Christ – tried as it sometimes is.[10]

The Anvil, The Fire And The Hammer

In his helpful book, *Genius, Grief and Grace*, Dr. Gaius Davies observes historically that "Many heroes, men and women of genius who achieved so much, did what they did in spite of much suffering." In fact, Dr. Davies observes that "many have said that their special trials and troubles enabled them to succeed in the way they did."[11]

Charles believed this too. Six years prior to his death, as he looked back over his life, he startles us with his perspective regarding the use of suffering to do good in life.

---

9   Charles Spurgeon, "A Prayer for Revival," *MTP*, Vol. 41 (Ages Digital Library, 1998), p. 518. See, "though I am told that I am a croaker, and too nervous, and so on."

10 Charles Spurgeon, "Witnesses Against You," *MTP*, Vol 36 (Ages Digital Library, 1998), p. 40.

11 Dr. Gaius Davies, *Genius, Grief & Grace: A Doctor Looks at Suffering & Success* (Scotland: Christian Focus, 2008), p. 13.

I am sure that I have run more swiftly with a lame leg than I ever did with a sound one. I am certain that I have seen more in the dark than ever I saw in the light, – more stars, most certainly, – more things in heaven if fewer things on earth. The anvil, the fire, and the hammer, are the making of us; we do not get fashioned much by anything else. That heavy hammer falling on us helps to shape us; therefore let affliction and trouble and trial come.[12]

In saying this, Charles sounds something like the apostle Paul who cried for relief but found none. Therefore he chose instead to boast in everything that was weak and lame about himself, discovering that the presence of God with him proved more blessed than the absence of his pains.

Charles therefore believed what some doubt; mainly, that the presence of evil does not require the absence of God. Even more, he believed that suffering can exist and God still be good; good both as God is in Himself and as God is toward us who suffer. In this faith, Charles found strength, conviction, endurance and refreshing joy, a peace that somehow transcended the peaceless pains he experienced.

He found his personal story in the stories of Biblical heroes who struggled with great trials such as Moses or Elijah, David or Paul. With Joseph, Charles would take up the words, "What was meant for evil, God intended for good" (to paraphrase Gen. 50:20). He believed that even the foulest choices of men and women could not disarm the good purpose of God from taking place in our lives.

---

12 Hayden, *Searchlight on Spurgeon*, p. 178.

In sum, Charles did not know why God allowed such things, but Charles did know to lean upon the presence of God within these allowances and also to derive the benefit that God would provide by them.

Good Doesn't Quit

In this light a new question joins the ancient one. We not only ask, "Why do bad things happen?" We also marvel and ask, "Why don't good things quit?" Charles accounts for many benefits in sorrows. These benefits outlast and ultimately triumph over our pain, misery and evil. Perhaps, as you read these benefits, you will not find yourself able to cherish them as Charles did. Don't let that stop you from meditating upon them. Perhaps in time some of them will become as dear to you as they once were to him.

Sorrow teaches us to resist trite views of what maturity in Jesus looks like: Faith is not frownless. Maturity is not painless. Disheveled and bedridden amid the jittery and unanswered; this is no necessary sign of wickedness. It is the presence of Jesus and not the absence of glee that designates the situation and provides our hope. Spurgeon says it this way: "Depression of spirit is no index of declining grace; the very loss of joy and the absence of assurance may be accompanied by the greatest advancement in the spiritual life ... we do not want rain all the days of the week, and all the weeks of the year; but if the rain comes sometimes, it makes the fields fertile, and fills the waterbrooks."[13]

Sorrows deepen our intimacy with God: When as children, "we were out at eventide walking with our father, we used sometimes to run on a long way ahead;

---

13 Spurgeon, "Sweet Stimulants for the Fainting Soul," (http://www.biblebb. com/files/spurgeon/2798.htm), accessed 3/25/14.

but, by-and-by, there was a big dog loose on the road, and it is astonishing how closely we clung to our father then."[14]

Charles can repeat the words of the Psalm 119 regarding the goodness, not of affliction itself, but of God's redeeming work within it. "I have found that there is a sweetness in bitterness not to be found in honey; a safety with Christ in a storm which may be lost in a calm. It is good for me that I have been afflicted."[15]

Likewise, he can testify from his pulpit regarding how his trials have actually increased his estimation of Jesus. "I have been seriously ill, and sadly depressed, and I fear I have rebelled, and therefore I look anew to him and I tell you that he is fairer in my eyes tonight than he was at first."[16]

Sorrows enable us to better receive blessings. "This very casting down in the dust sometimes enables the Christian to bear a blessing from God which he could not have carried if he had been standing upright. There is such a thing as being crushed with a load of grace, bowed down with a tremendous weight of benedictions, having such blessings from God that, if our soul were not cast down by them, they would be the ruin of us."[17]

Sorrows shed our pretences: Sorrow unthreads the hem of our rationalizations. Spurgeon says, "When this down-casting comes, it gets us to work at self-examination .... When your house has been made to shake, it has caused you to see whether it was founded upon a rock."[18]

---

14   Spurgeon, "Sweet Stimulants for the Fainting Soul."

15   Hayden, *Searchlight on Spurgeon*, p. 185.

16   ibid., p. 184.

17   Spurgeon, "Sweet Stimulants for the Fainting Soul," p. 580.

18   Spurgeon, "Sweet Stimulants for the Fainting Soul, (http://www.biblebb.com/files/spurgeon/2798.htm), accessed 3/25/14.

Sorrow exposes and roots out our pride: Perhaps we can think of it this way. When standing at a thrift sale, the saying goes, "One man's garbage is another man's treasure." We often mix-up what Jesus treasures with what Jesus willingly gets rid of. Sorrows reveal where we've been wide eyed for brand new nothings and overlooked old treasures. "We are very apt to grow too big," Spurgeon says. "It is a good thing for us to be taken down a notch or two. We sometimes rise too high, in our own estimation, that unless the Lord took away some of our joy, we should be utterly destroyed by pride."[19]

Sorrow teaches us empathy for one another: Spurgeon says, "If we had never been in trouble ourselves, we should be very poor comforters of others .... It would be no disadvantage to a surgeon if he once knew what it was to have a broken bone; you may depend upon it that his touch would be more tender afterwards; he would not be so rough with his patients as he might have been if he had never felt such pain himself."[20]

Sorrows allow small kindnesses to loom large. "You know, dear brothers and sisters, how a little act of kindness will lift us when we are very low in spirit ... even a tender look from a child will help to remove our depression. In times of loneliness, it is something even to have a dog with you, to lick your hand, and show you such kindness as is possible from him."[21]

Sorrows teach us courage for others who face trials. "And you timid, nervous people, have you not found out for

19   ibid.

20   ibid.

21   Charles Spurgeon, "The Weakened Christ, Strengthened," M*TP*, Vol. 48 (Ages Digital Library, 1998), p. 148.

yourselves that, if ever you get into an accident, you are often the bravest people there? You feeble trembling ones seem strengthened up at the moment."[22]

Conclusion

Sorrows are caused by ugly things. But Jesus adopts them as it were. He brings them into His own counsel. The One who loves even enemies puts our sorrows on probation. He gives them His own heart and provision and house. Living with Him they reform and take on His purposes to promote His intentions. In Him, they reverse and thwart foul tidings.

In other words, our sorrows belong to Jesus. He is their master no matter what fiendish thought or unexplainable cause gave them birth. Jesus shows us His wounds, the slanders, the manipulations, the injustices, the body blows, the mistreatments piled on to Him. From there He loves, still. He invites us into fellowship with His empathy. We receive it from Him in the deeps.

Charles cherished a certain picture. The engraver portrayed the moment in *Pilgrim's Progress* in which Christian panics, swallowed up by the deeps of a river and going under. The portrait shows Christian's companion, named Hopeful, pushing up with his arm around Christian and lifting up his hands shouting, "Fear not! Brother, I feel the bottom."

With this picture on his mind, the preacher so familiar with sorrows then rejoices with those listening to him. "This is just what Jesus does in our trials," Charles proclaims. "He puts his arm around us, points up and

---

22 Charles Spurgeon, "Refusing to Be Comforted," *MTP*, Vol. 44 (Ages Digital Library, 1998), p. 417.

says, 'Fear not! The water may be deep, but the bottom is good.'"[23]

> It may be, that you suffer from a mental sickness in the form of depression of spirit. Things look very dark, and your heart is very heavy.... When life is like a foggy day—when providence is cloudy and stormy, and you are caught in a hurricane.... When your soul is exceedingly sorrowful, and you are bruised as a cluster trodden in the wine-press, yet cling close to God, and never let go of your reverent fear of him. However exceptional and unusual may be your trial, yet, with Job whisper these words, "Though he slay me, yet will I trust him."[24]

In such whispers, often unheard and unnoticed, His treasures shine as it were, small but warm like a candle flame within a cracked jar. Invaluable this flicker amid the howling winds of night's deep. His vigil light, undaunted, keeps watch over the helpless, keeps watch through to the morning. The sun may not rise for a few hours yet. But here amid the waiting hours, the sorrowing have a Savior.

---

23   Hayden, *Searchlight on Spurgeon*, p. 185.

24   Charles Spurgeon, "All the Day Long," *MTP*, Vol. 36 (Ages Digital Library, 1998), p. 433.

Christian Focus Publications

Our mission statement –

STAYING FAITHFUL
In dependence upon God we seek to impact the world through literature faithful to His infallible Word, the Bible. Our aim is to ensure that the Lord Jesus Christ is presented as the only hope to obtain forgiveness of sin, live a useful life and look forward to heaven with Him.

Our books are published in four imprints:

CHRISTIAN
FOCUS

Popular works including biographies, commentaries, basic doctrine and Christian living.

CHRISTIAN
HERITAGE

Books representing some of the best material from the rich heritage of the church.

MENTOR

Books written at a level suitable for Bible College and seminary students, pastors, and other serious readers. The imprint includes commentaries, doctrinal studies, examination of current issues and church history.

CF4•K

Children's books for quality Bible teaching and for all age groups: Sunday school curriculum, puzzle and activity books; personal and family devotional titles, biographies and inspirational stories – because you are never too young to know Jesus!

Christian Focus Publications Ltd,
Geanies House, Fearn, Ross-shire,
IV20 1TW, Scotland, United Kingdom.
www.christianfocus.com